bellissima!

The Italian Automotive Renaissance
1945–1975

Published in conjunction with the exhibition
Bellissima! The Italian Automotive Renaissance, 1945–1975,
organized by the Frist Center for the Visual Arts, Nashville,
May 27–October 9, 2016

PRESENTING SPONSORS
Barbara, Jack, Sara, and Richard Bovender

PLATINUM SPONSOR

SUPPORTING SPONSOR

MEDIA SPONSOR

The Frist Center for the Visual Arts is supported in part by

The Frist Center gratefully acknowledges the Friends
of Italian Art.

Library of Congress Control Number: 2015959528
ISBN: 978-0-8478-4751-8

First published in the United States of America in 2016 by

Skira Rizzoli Publications, Inc.
300 Park Avenue South
New York, NY 10010
rizzoliusa.com

in association with

Frist Center for the Visual Arts
919 Broadway
Nashville, TN 37203
fristcenter.org

Designed by MGMT. design

For Skira Rizzoli Publications, Inc.:
Charles Miers, Publisher
Margaret Rennolds Chace, Associate Publisher
Ellen Cohen, Editor

For the Frist Center for the Visual Arts:
Wallace Joiner, Managing Editor
Peg Duthie, Editor

Printed in China

2016 2017 2018 2019 / 10 9 8 7 6 5 4 3 2 1

Cover: 1953 Alfa Romeo BAT 5. The Blackhawk Collection.
Photo © 2016 Peter Harholdt

bellissima!

The Italian Automotive Renaissance
1945–1975

KEN GROSS

ROBERT CUMBERFORD

WINSTON GOODFELLOW

PRINCIPAL PHOTOGRAPHY BY
PETER HARHOLDT

contents

foreword

Susan H. Edwards, PhD
Executive Director and CEO, Frist Center for the Visual Arts

Encouraged by the enthusiastic response to our 2013 exhibition *Sensuous Steel: Art Deco Automobiles*, we began discussing then the possibility of hosting another exhibition devoted to vehicle design. Art Deco automobiles were an obvious connection to the historic architecture of the Frist Center, and the exhibition succeeded on many levels. It enticed some people to an art museum for the first time and brought back local residents who had not been inside 919 Broadway since it was Nashville's main post office. Visitors quickly grasped the relevance of automobile design in the context of our Art Deco home; as well as the inspiration for the exhibition, good design is something we encounter in our everyday lives. *Sensuous Steel* also sparked a civic discussion about honoring the city's architectural past as the community experiences a construction boom. In August 2013, we hosted our initial Art Deco Affair: proceeds from the annual party and ongoing donations to the Art Deco Society are devoted to the care of our building, which is owned by the Metropolitan Development Housing Agency (MDHA) and maintained by the Frist Center.

When we approached Ken Gross, who had served as guest curator of *Sensuous Steel*, about organizing another automobile exhibition for the Frist Center, he immediately proposed a study of postwar Italian vehicles. He explained that the post–World War II economic recovery of Italy from near devastation to international economic power was due, in part, to the automotive industry. The idea of an exhibition exploring the design of Italian automobiles was appealing to us. Soon afterward, Ken began planning *Bellissima! The Italian Automotive Renaissance, 1945–1975*. In recent years, Ken, a former director of the Petersen Automotive Museum, in Los Angeles, has become the foremost curator of automobile exhibitions in the country. We are extremely pleased to work with him again and are grateful that he has called on his extensive contacts and goodwill to locate and secure nineteen automobiles and three motorcycles whose excellence in design and craftsmanship demonstrate some of the reasons Italian vehicles stood out among their North American, European, and Japanese competitors.

The Frist Center's connections to Italian design may appear less direct than our debt to the Art Deco movement, but they are no less potent. We have hosted major exhibitions on Italian painting, sculpture, drawing, glass, and fashion, bringing to the community masterpieces by artists from Michelangelo to Missoni. Several years ago we launched the Friends of Italian Art, a support group of like-minded patrons who continue to encourage further exposure to the rich Italian culture. Italian automobiles are synonymous with elegance, prestige, and sex appeal. Their allure attracts men and women in equal measure. We are drawn to their sophisticated design, precision engineering, and luxurious interiors, as well as the association of Italian automobiles with the glamour of racing, Hollywood, and royalty. *Bellissima!* adds another dimension to our understanding of the irrepressible creative spirit of Italy while delighting us visually, sensually, and intellectually.

We want to express our sincere gratitude to the lenders whose generosity was essential to the project. For sharing their exquisite vehicles we thank: Peter Matthew Calles, Bethesda, Maryland; Bernard and Joan Carl, Washington, D.C.; the Luigi Chinetti Trust, Stuart, Florida; Miles Collier, president, and Scott George, vice president, The Revs Institute for Automotive Research, Inc., Naples, Florida; The Gilbert Family, Los Angeles; Paul Gould, Patterson, New York; Scott Grundfor and Kathleen Redmond, Arroyo Grande, California; Somer and Loyce Hooker, Brentwood, Tennessee; Thomas Mao, advisor, the XJ Wang Collection, Los Angeles; Don and Diane Meluzio, York, Pennsylvania; Christopher Ohrstrom, The Plains, Virginia; James E. Petersen Jr., Houston; Linda and Bill Pope, Paradise Valley, Arizona; Brandt Rosenbusch, historical services manager, Fiat Chrysler Automobiles (FCA), Auburn Hills, Michigan; David Sydorick, Beverly Hills; Morrie Wagener, CEO, Morrie's Classic Cars, LLC, Long Lake, Minnesota; and Don Williams, president, The Blackhawk Collection, Danville, California.

Many people were indispensable during the organization of the exhibition. For their assistance in helping us secure loans and for attending to important details, we gratefully acknowledge: Ed Brown, Tow Guy, Van Nuys, California; Bruce Canepa, Canepa Motorsports Museum, Scotts Valley, California; Angela Day, associate registrar, Indianapolis Museum of Art; Webb Farrar; Elaine Fichtel, executive assistant to Morrie Wagener; Richard Gadeselli, chairman, Fiat Chrysler Automobiles Services UK Ltd., London; David Grainger, The Guild of Automotive Restorers, Bradford, Ontario; Rich Heinrich,

Scottsdale (Arizona) Automotive Museum; Terry Karges, executive director, and Leslie Kendall, curator, Petersen Automotive Museum; Bruce Meyer, Beverly Hills; Jayme Moore, executive assistant/office manager, The Revs Institute for Automotive Research, Inc.; and Frederick A. Simeone, executive director, and Kevin Kelly, curator, Simeone Foundation and Automotive Museum, Philadelphia.

It is a great honor to copublish *Bellissima! The Italian Automotive Renaissance, 1945–1975* with Skira Rizzoli Publications. We are pleased to be associated with their reputation for design excellence and that the catalogue will bear their renowned name. For his early support we acknowledge Charles Miers, publisher, Rizzoli Publications. We also thank Margaret Rennolds Chace, associate publisher, Skira Rizzoli Publications; Ellen Cohen, senior editor, Rizzoli Publications; and copyeditor Tanya Heinrich. For his inestimable aptitude for capturing beauty and grace in three dimensions, we thank photographer Peter Harholdt. We are likewise grateful to Michael Furman and to Joe Wiecha for additional photography for this catalogue. For their intelligent catalogue entries on Italian vehicles, we thank Ken Gross, Robert Cumberford, and Winston Goodfellow. Ken Gross is the driving force behind the exhibition and catalogue. His introductory essay here sets the stage and tone for both.

At the Frist Center, we gratefully acknowledge chief curator Mark Scala. We thank him for his intelligence, generosity of spirit, and good humor in addressing the needs of a guest curator while never allowing the ball to drop on various other departmental responsibilities. Wallace Joiner, managing editor and registrar, is comparable to a precision driving machine—always

dependable and able to maneuver in tight spots while anticipating sudden curves ahead. We thank her for her diligence and attention to detail. For additional assistance and scrutiny we thank line editor Peg Duthie. We also thank Amie Geremia, head registrar, and Scott Thom, chief preparator, and his team, for all they did to get the vehicles here and installed beautifully. We thank exhibition designer Michael Brechner and senior designer Hans Schmitt-Matzen for their commitment to all projects, but especially for their stylish mise-en-scène for *Bellissima!* Phil El Rassi designed the exhibition graphics in perfect harmony. We thank Michael, Hans, and Phil for their visual realization of Ken's ideas.

Neither the exhibition nor this publication would be possible without the generous support of sponsors. It is rare to have the funders on board while an exhibition is still in the concept phase, but that is the moment when knowing that it will be possible is most critical. We are indebted to Barbara and Jack Bovender for their early encouragement. Special thanks are due to Barbara, Jack, Sara, and Richard Bovender for their generous financial commitment to the presentation of *Bellissima!* at the Frist Center. We also thank the HCA Foundation on behalf of HCA and TriStar Health for their continuing support. Our sincere appreciation goes as well to CHUBB Insurance, *Sports Car Digest*, and the Friends of Italian Art. For ongoing general operating support we acknowledge with gratitude the Metro Nashville Arts Commission, the Tennessee Arts Commission, and the National Endowment for the Arts. As always, we thank the Frist Foundation and the Frist Center Board of Trustees, especially Billy Frist, president. Finally, we acknowledge again Ken Gross, who has taught us that a car is never just a car.

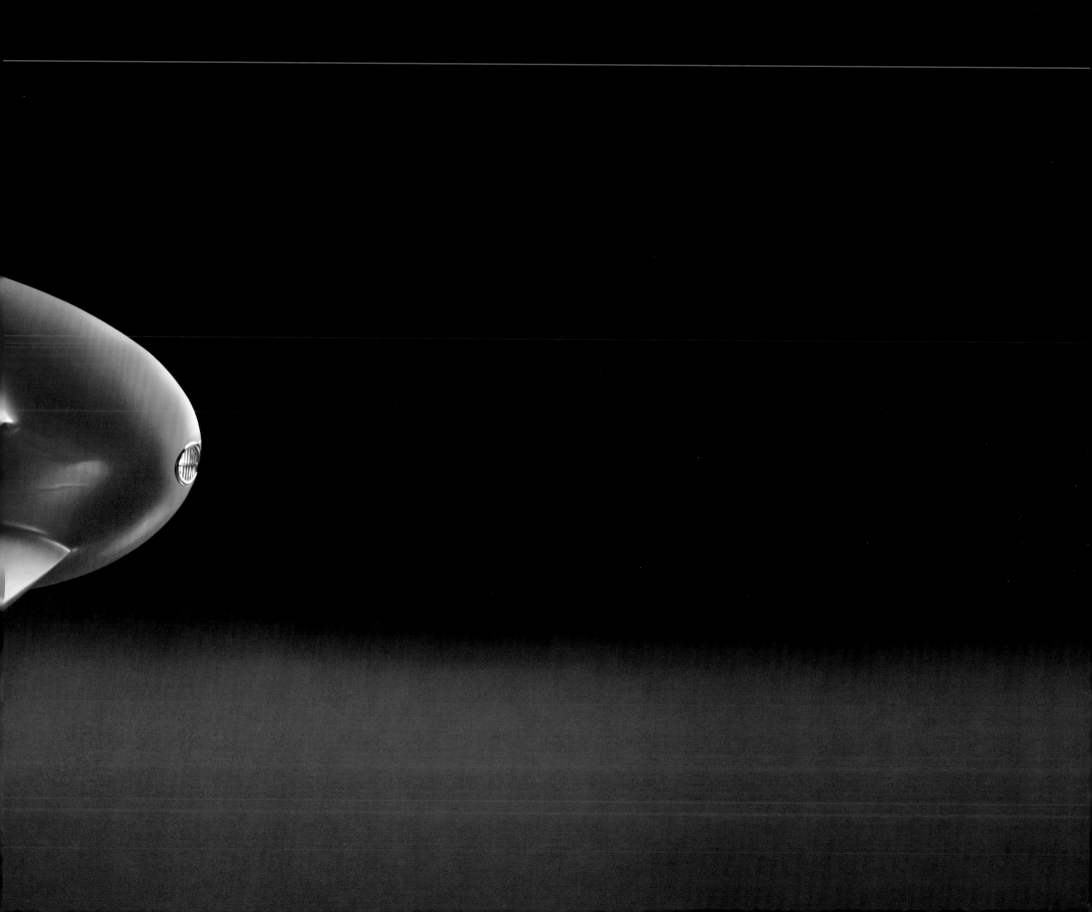

FIG. 1. The 52nd fire brigade, Milan, Via de Castilla,
Tecnomasio Italiano, February 14, 1943

"A GIANT COMPRESSED SPRING": ITALY'S POSTWAR AUTOMOTIVE RENAISSANCE *Ken Gross*

Post–World War II Italy witnessed a remarkable industrial and cultural rebirth known as the Italian economic miracle (*il miracolo economico*). This encompassed world-acclaimed fashion, film, graphic design, and furniture design; advanced aeronautics; sleek watercraft; and the subject of this catalogue and exhibition, spectacular automobiles and motorcycles.

Badly damaged during the final years of the conflict (fig. 1), Italy's manufacturing and design capabilities had reached a nadir by 1945. But the country's indomitable creative spirit—the inspiration for its art and architecture for centuries—thankfully remained intact. Even as the war raged on, Alfa Romeo assembled a few 6C 2500 sports cars, which were completed, often with custom coachwork, for high government officials and wealthy, influential civilians.

Meanwhile, unable to build the futuristic cars and motorcycles of their dreams, Italian auto designers fantasized about what they would do when hostilities ceased. Research for the war effort helped Italian engineers and designers become very familiar with the principles of applied aeronautics, lightweight body construction, and streamlining, as well as the use of sophisticated materials such as aluminum and magnesium, of powerful and high-revving aircraft engines, and of other military necessities that could be translated into automotive luxuries.

Unlike the Japanese (who did not have a substantial automotive history before the war) or the Americans (whose automobile industry, the aptly named "Arsenal of Democracy," had been totally converted over to wartime production and was thus slow to offer totally new postwar car designs), the Italians had proven coachbuilders (*carrozzerie*, *carrozzerias*, or *carrozieri*) and a long prewar history of sports and racing car competition successes. Thus, as their country began its recovery, existing automakers were able to quickly reestablish production, while new companies like Cisitalia and Ferrari used the resumption of auto racing as a platform to begin producing stylish, highly advanced road-going cars of great merit. In the words of the designer Filippo Sapino, the Italian car industry "was like a giant compressed spring" by the end of World War II, with the arrival of peace releasing its pent-up energy.[1]

In *The Art of the Sports Car*, author Dennis Adler quotes a poignant statement from Alfa Romeo that sums up how that proud firm felt in 1946: "The roar of the destroying war had just ceased from the skies, but down on earth a new roar is rising . . . a song of revival [that] announces that peaceful men are at work again. The works, which still bear the war scars, are already teeming with new life, and the new Alfa Romeos are fanning out towards the roads of the world which again will be paved with their victories." The poetic declaration concluded, "The renowned Alfa Romeo works offer proof of the reviving Italian industry, as well as an ingenious combination of mechanical perfection."[2]

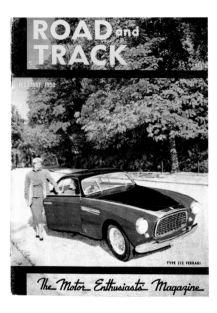

At the same time, Italian coachbuilders such as Allemano, Boano, Frua, Ghia, Pinin Farina, Touring, and Vignale drew on metal-shaping techniques that can be traced back to those of armorers in the Middle Ages. With this combination of centuries-old skill and new creative energy, they began to build limited-production car bodies for Italian domestic manufacturers. They were cost efficient because of low labor rates, and quick to respond to the demands of American carmakers, helping those manufacturers build some of the most beautiful concept cars ever created, as well as attractive bodies for American and European production cars. By the early 1950s, the world was turning to Italy for advanced automotive design.

The vehicles in *Bellissima! The Italian Automotive Renaissance, 1945–1975* were carefully chosen to showcase many of the best cars and motorcycles from the postwar period. The individual entries in this catalogue speak to the brilliance of Italian design and engineering innovation and their influence on the world. This essay offers a brief overview of the cars and motorcycles in the exhibition, leaving it to readers and exhibition visitors to discover the intriguing nuances and avant-garde elements that distinguish each of these machines.

up from the ashes

Before 1940 Italy's economy had been largely agrarian, and its postwar renaissance did not come easily. The country's many unemployed soldiers and displaced civilians faced a devastated landscape, a crumbling infrastructure, and the presence of the Communist Party in the newly elected Italian government. Fortunately, the US Marshall Plan provided a healthy injection of funds to jump-start Italy's struggling economy, which helped stave off both fiscal collapse and revolutionary discord.

At first, Italy was regarded more as an enemy than a friend by the winning side. In 1946 Gian Battista "Pinin" Farina brought one of the cars in this exhibition to the first postwar Salon de l'Automobile in Paris.[3] His presence was not welcome; his entry was denied, despite his epic six-hundred-kilometer drive from Lausanne, forcing him to display his new car *outside* the Auto Salon. Luckily, the cognoscenti recognized the brilliance of his design, and the Salon organizers allowed him entry the following year. (Pinin Farina and the carrozzeria bearing his name would eventually become so renowned that in 1961, as a gesture of honor from the president of Italy, both the family and company names were changed to Pininfarina. We thus use both Pinin Farina and Pininfarina in discussing the achievements of the founder and his firm.)

Competition on road courses and tracks resumed surprisingly quickly after the war. The Mille Miglia, Italy's famed thousand-mile road race (held on public

highways from Brescia to Rome and back to Brescia), attracted huge crowds and international entries, contributing to a renewed spirit of Italian racing success against tough competitors from Europe and North America. Piero Dusio's company, Cisitalia, began its existence with fast, lightweight race cars, and then produced a Carrozzeria Pinin Farina–built, Fiat-powered Model 202 sports coupe designed by Giovanni Savonuzzi with chassis work by Fiat's Dante Giacosa. Its dramatically streamlined shape captivated audiences wherever it was shown.

The Cisitalia 202 is an important inclusion in this exhibition. Arthur Drexler, a curator of architecture at New York City's Museum of Modern Art, and curator of MoMA's unprecedented 1951 exhibition *8 Automobiles*, praised this sleek new model, saying, "The Cisitalia's body is slipped over its chassis like a dust jacket over a book. . . . Because the sloping hood lies between the two front fenders, it suggests low, fast power."[4] MoMA

went on to acquire a Cisitalia 202—the first car in its permanent collection—and has exhibited it from time to time over many years (fig. 4). While just 170 were sold (Cisitalia 202s were relatively expensive), the design had an extraordinary effect on car buyers and automakers alike, inspiring the Maserati A6G 1500 and a host of other imitators. Designer and critic Robert Cumberford wrote, "It is astonishing that the coupes have had such an enormous influence on car design."[5]

In the postwar period, sleek, technically advanced jet aircraft and rockets were considered the most modern and spectacular examples of streamlining and contemporary engineering. Soon, styling cues from the air began to influence automobiles on the roads.

Fiat, which commonly built affordable mass-produced cars, offered a small series of advanced sports coupes and roadsters. Each Otto Vu (Fiat 8V) was powered by a little jewel of a two-liter, eight-cylinder engine. The most exciting of the 144 produced were the Supersonics,

which were clad in futuristic, aircraft-inspired aluminum bodies styled by Ghia's very talented Giovanni Savonuzzi (fig. 6). Jet aircraft cues abound, from an elegantly long hood, a snug cockpit, and pointy rear fenders that resemble jet afterburners, to side strakes and elongated side vents. Viewed from any angle, a Supersonic is still absolutely stunning more than sixty years after it was created. Just twenty were built—sixteen on Fiat 8V chassis, one on an Aston Martin DB2/4 platform, and three on Jaguar XKs. Today, 8V Supersonics are seven-figure cars that rarely change hands.

Italy's innovative Vincenzo Lancia pioneered sliding pillar suspensions, narrow-angle V-6 engines, unit-body construction, and a host of other technical firsts. Lancia offered exquisite sports models that attracted the best coachbuilders. In 1952 Pininfarina showed a Lancia PF 200 Spyder at the Salone dell'automobile di Torino, which was followed by a coupe at the Paris Salon. The distinct aircraft influence on these cars could be seen in the

rounded grilles, which suggested jet intakes, as well as in their projectile-like shapes and elegantly tapered rears. Lancia went on to build a lovely series of Aurelia spiders and B20 coupes that were equally at home touring the Alps or rallying to Monte Carlo, producing them until 1958.

In North America, Chrysler's conservative chairman, Kaufmann Thuma "K. T." Keller, had insisted that his cars be practical—which, to him, meant upright, boxy, and staid. When the company's postwar sales volume stalled, a desperate Keller hired Virgil M. Exner, who had a bright imagination and the ability to inspire contemporaries. Exner was ready to challenge the irrepressible and highly successful Harley J. Earl and his acclaimed Art and Color staff at General Motors. Exner's ace in this dogfight was Carrozzeria Ghia, where Luigi Segre and Giovanni Savonuzzi produced a dazzling series of "idea cars" that inspired a production design theme called "The Forward Look." Strident Plymouth advertisements

in 1957 blared, "Suddenly it's 1960!" and displayed new model cars with crisp, bold, elegant shapes inspired by Exner's "Italian connection." Even better, and despite the transatlantic freight fees, Ghia could build stunning show cars faster and more economically than anyone in Detroit or Los Angeles. Exner was called a "Visioneer," a now quaint but very descriptive moniker.[6]

Sadly, one dramatic Ghia idea car, the Chrysler Norseman (fig. 7), was lost forever when the SS *Andrea Doria* sank on its one hundredth Atlantic crossing, en route from Italy to the United States. The stunning Norseman boasted a razor-thin windscreen, a huge, cantilevered fastback roof, sweeping fender lines, and prominent fins. Its striking presence, which really showed the breadth of Exner's stylistic direction, survives only in a few photographs.

The most exciting Ghia confection was arguably an arrow-shaped *berlinetta* (small, sporty coupe) whose pointy aircraft-inspired fins had been wind tunnel tested

at Politecnico di Torino (Polytechnic University of Turin) to prove that they could positively affect the car's stability at high speeds. Once again, the design genius of Savonuzzi was in play. Exner had reportedly shown his Italian cohorts a small, dramatically shaped model car for inspiration; the four-wheeled result, named for Rita Hayworth and her role in *Gilda*, a popular film noir, evoked a sexy and feminine Hollywood vision, but with enough aircraft hints to be considered ultramodern for its time (fig. 8). The Gilda was originally slated to be powered by a small gasoline engine, but when it was restored, the car received a period gas turbine power plant. With its muted jet-like whine, this engine better suited the Gilda's jet-like shape.

FIG. 7. 1956 Chrysler Norseman

america joins in

After the war ended, the newly resurrected Italian carrozzerie were intrigued by the huge, financially booming
American market. Ghia produced a pair of elegant
coupes on the Cadillac 60 Special chassis (fig. 9), as
well as the concept cars for Chrysler discussed in the
previous section. Carrozzeria Vignale presented a
one-off convertible for Packard, and built the bodies
for Briggs Cunningham's brutish, Hemi-powered C3
cabriolets and berlinettas.[7] Carrozzeria Touring hand-
built a series of twenty-six Hudson Italias on Hudson
Jet chassis. Pininfarina was retained by Nash to design
production Airflyte coupe and sedan bodies. The
features of Felice Mario Boano's Indianapolis luxury
coupe (fig. 10) were inspired by the sleek shapes of jet
fighter aircraft; while it never influenced the design
of production Lincolns, it was a bold achievement
for the period.[8] When an American carmaker wanted
something special and classy, it gave the commission
to an Italian coachbuilder.

To demonstrate its engineering prowess, Fiat
developed a gas turbine car. Built by hand in Fiat's
experimental shop in 1954, this one-of-a-kind car was
called *La Turbina*. Designed by Fabio Luigi Rapi, the Fiat
Turbine boasted a surrealistic scallop paint job, a tiny
cockpit with a semipanoramic windscreen, fins that were
nearly one-third of the car's length, and a large, round,
centered exhaust that resembled a fighter aircraft's.
Britain's Rover built an experimental jet car around the
same time, and General Motors' Firebird I concept car
had anticipated both of these efforts, but it was left to
Chrysler, with help from Ghia, to make the Turbine Car
a reality (fig. 11).[9]

After Virgil Exner left Chrysler, Elwood Engel was
recruited from Ford Motor Company to take Chrysler to
the next level. At this point Chrysler was considering
gas turbine power plants for its road cars. Drawing on
his Ford Thunderbird design for inspiration, Engel was
responsible for the Chrysler Turbine Car as well as one
of the most unusual testing schemes ever devised by
a carmaker. Some fifty-five identical Chrysler Turbines
were handcrafted in Italy by Carrozzeria Ghia, all in a
coppery orange hue. Over time, fifty of those cars were
loaned to several hundred families to test on US public
roads. Chrysler technicians traveled around the United
States to ensure that the cars were operating well and
to facilitate the transfers from family to family. But, after
another round of testing a more advanced version, the
threat of emissions regulations and poor fuel economy
ended the experiment. Legal, product liability, and
import tax issues drove Chrysler to destroy nearly all of
the cars, leaving just nine in the hands of museums and
private individuals.[10]

Giuseppe "Nuccio" Bertone was another inspired
Italian design house chief. Raised in the business by
his father, Giovanni Bertone, Nuccio was always deeply

FIG. 11. 1963 Chrysler Turbine Car in Australia, one of the stops on its world tour of twenty-one countries via PanAm

FIG. 12. From left to right, 1953 Alfa Romeo BAT 5, 1954 Alfa Romeo BAT 7, and 1955 Alfa Romeo BAT 9

involved with his firm's designs, and he had a great eye for talent. He may be best remembered for a striking trio of show cars for Alfa Romeo that have never quite been imitated. Alfa engineers wanted to research the coefficient of drag (Cd) for motor vehicles. From 1953 to 1955 they commissioned Carrozzeria Bertone to build three futuristic low-drag cars, to be called BAT (Berlinetta Aerodinamica Tecnica), for the Turin Auto Show.

Built on Alfa 1900 chassis, and despite having only seventy-five- to one-hundred-bhp (brake horsepower) four-cylinder engines, the astonishing BATs (fig. 12) were capable of speeds up to 125 mph. All three prototype BATs were styled by the very talented Franco Scaglione, who would later design several significant Italian milestone cars. The BATs featured prominently rounded "noses," deep horizontal front air scoops, virtually enclosed front wheels (for better aerodynamics), and curvaceous fins and tapered tails (for high-speed stability). Each car was more advanced than its predecessor.

The best Cd achieved was 0.19, a figure only recently matched with a production model.

All three BATs were aerodynamically efficient, daring, and unforgettable, and their audacity inspired other designers to think more boldly. Viewed together, most often at the Blackhawk Museum in Danville, California, these three advanced berlinettas are remarkable creations. Alfa Romeo went on to attract coachbuilders to the chassis it developed after the Model 1900. Many lovely prototypes and production cars were coachbuilt by styling firms such as Ghia, Pininfarina, Touring, Zagato, and others, but none were as outrageous or sexy as the BATs.

racing led the way

Enzo Ferrari organized and managed Scuderia Ferrari, the official Alfa Romeo racing team, before the Second

World War, but he had a personality conflict with Wilfredo Ricart, a Spanish engineer hired by Alfa Romeo. Ricart's designs, while brilliantly conceived, were often not practical or track proficient, and Ferrari left after a dispute. As part of his severance agreement with Alfa Romeo, Ferrari was unable to use his own name for four years, so for the 1940 Mille Miglia he entered a pair of newly built cars under the name AAV (Auto Avio Costruzioni). During the war, his company, which manufactured machine tools, had been heavily bombed. After hostilities ended, Ferrari resumed using his own name, building race cars powered by small-displacement but high-revving twelve-cylinder engines. Ferrari's small initial staff included Gioachino Colombo, a brilliant engineer who had worked for Alfa Romeo before the war.

Racing was very expensive, especially in an era when sponsorship was just beginning to make supportive contributions. Encouraged by former racer and 24 Heures

du Mans (24 Hours of Le Mans) winner Luigi Chinetti Sr., his colleague and principal contact in North America, Ferrari began to offer road-going chassis. He retained Italy's finest carrozzerie to custom-build beautiful, sexy cars that immediately caught the attention of wealthy glitterati, cinema stars, and influential industrialists. These notables relished the idea of exclusive, attention-drawing automobiles equipped with powerful engines and distinguished by their racing reputation, advanced engineering, and styling. Ferrari used their patronage, as well as displays of his cars at major auto shows (despite a limited promotional budget), to help publicize the new marque (fig. 13). The irrepressible Chinetti, who financed Ferrari's initial sales efforts with his own funds, found that the combination of racing success and highbrow clientele helped him popularize Ferraris in North America.

The earliest road-going Ferraris, never built in high numbers, were succeeded by small series production

models developed by Carrozzeria Touring with its patented Superleggera construction method, where artisans shaped and stretched thin sheets of aluminum over a framework of small tubing. Touring hand-built the exquisite Ferrari Barchetta models, one of which, driven by Luigi Chinetti Sr., won the 24 Hours of Le Mans in 1949, instantly establishing Ferrari automobiles as world contenders. Alfredo Vignale's shop also created a number of distinctive custom bodies on early Ferraris, including a special series of five berlinettas distinguished by vestigial fins and small double bumpers.

Pinin Farina assumed most of Ferrari's coachbuilding by the end of the 1950s. Ferrari wanted a distinct look for his cars, and although he could choose from any coachbuilder in the world, he and Farina had a famous meeting in Tortona, a town located between Turin and Maranello, that resulted in a lifelong partnership. Reflecting on the momentous meeting, Farina said, "The fact is that Ferrari and I both wanted to get the automobile away from the

melodramatic, the monumental, even the visionary, and quit the decorative forever."[11]

Ferrari's 250 GT chassis was armed with a powerful three-liter V-12 and produced as much as three hundred bhp in a race-prepared "SEFAC Hot Rod" 250 short-wheel-base berlinetta (SWB) configuration. It would reach its front-engine peak with the 250 GTO (fig. 14). Just thirty-six of these swift berlinettas were built with three-liter engines. Three 330 GTOs were fitted with four-liter V-12s. The curvaceous and minimalist body design was attributed to Sergio Scaglietti, whose shop in Modena constructed the model's sleek body shells (and also did work for Pininfarina). Ferrari earmarked these select competition cars for official factory drivers and talented private competitors. One couldn't just purchase a new GTO; you had to be *somebody*. Engineered by Giotto Bizzarrini, with bodies by Carrozzeria Scaglietti, and virtually unbeatable by any rival with a similar-sized engine, the lithe, lightweight GTOs, when skillfully

driven, could take the measure of much larger race cars. Today, the rare and lovely Ferrari GTO is the single most valuable vintage automobile extant. Examples have sold for over fifty million dollars each.

Before long, Ferrari's regular customers could choose from a variety of elegant high-performance road cars. The very wealthy and successful could special-order the 410 Superamerica, with custom coachwork by Pininfarina, with open or covered headlights and a variety of interior trim specifications. Built from 1956 to 1959 in three series, these big road-burners were powerful (with up to four hundred bhp), rare, exclusive, and very fast. They were succeeded by the more aerodynamic 400 Superamerica (fig. 15) from 1960 to 1964. As with the 410s, no two 400 SAs were exactly alike. Disc brakes were now part of the specification, as well as a four-speed gearbox and overdrive. Former *Road & Track* editor Dean Batchelor wrote, "Traveling in a Superamerica was traveling in style. The owners knew it and all who saw the car knew it, which

is what the owners wanted them to know."[12] The 400 SA in this exhibition was built to order for the Riva family, makers of Italy's finest speedboats and yachts.

Ferrari patrons and clientele included movie producer Roberto Rossellini and his wife, Ingrid Bergman (who owned six Ferraris over time); the founder of Superior Oil Company, Howard Keck; toilet tissue magnate and early Ferrari racer Jim Kimberly; King Farouk I of Egypt; Belgium's King Leopold; the Aga Kahn; the Los Angeles playboy Tommy Lee; Henry Ford II; America's Cup yachtsman, racer, and car manufacturer Briggs Cunningham; and, not surprisingly, Fiat chief Gianni Agnelli. This *Who's Who* list of Ferrari owners goes on and on. These owners and others helped establish Ferrari as a very prestigious brand, in part by commissioning coachbuilt cars and appearing with these cars at exclusive events. Some celebrity owners even raced in competitions, until the cars became too fast for nonprofessional drivers.

Despite the company's success in racing and its spectacular road cars, life was not harmonious at Ferrari. After a personal dispute in the early 1960s involving Ferrari's contentious wife, Laura, and popular sales manager Girolamo Gardini, Ferrari lost brilliant engineers Giotto Bizzarrini, Carlo Chiti, Romolo Tavoni, and several other employees almost overnight, including driver Phil Hill, the 1961 Formula 1 world champion. Backed by industrialist Giorgio Billi, Bolivian tin fortune heir Jaime Ortiz-Patino, and successful racer Count Giovanni Volpi, who ran Scuderia Serenissima, these "walkouts" quickly formed a new company called ATS (Automobili Turismo e Sport) to build racing cars and road-going sports models. Their stunning retort was the radical new ATS 2500 GT: it featured a midmounted V-8 engine, an engineering step Ferrari was reluctant to take. (He did not offer a large-displacement mid-engine road car because he believed that they were too dangerous for his customers.) The ATS 2500 GT (fig. 17) took its first

FIG. 17. 1963 ATS 2500 GT brochure

FIG. 18. 1964 Lamborghini 350 GT brochure

bow at the Salon international de l'automobile de Genève (Geneva Motor Show) in 1963. It received rave reviews from respected testers, and many initial orders, but the innovative yet hastily developed ATS was not ready for production and the company was underfunded: very few 2500 GTs were produced before this magnificent failure passed from the scene.

Ferrari's key Italian rival for many years was Maserati, a sporting make that began in 1913 and was eager to build attractive, performance-oriented roadsters and berlinettas. With its highways repaired, the autostradas and autobahns beckoning, and the world economy growing, premier Italian automakers sought to satisfy an expanding desire for high-performance cars. Maserati introduced the A6GCS racer, designed by Gioachino Colombo, formerly with Ferrari. Maserati's two-liter twin-cam sixes, independent front suspension, and tubular chassis followed contemporary Italian practice, but the combination was perfectly balanced and very capable.

Coachbuilders were attracted to the marque, and designs by Frua, Pininfarina, and Vignale soon followed. For the road, the more mildly tuned A6G was an ideal platform, especially with lightweight double-bubble coachwork by Zagato. The famed "Birdcage" Maserati race car, with a chassis formed from a labyrinth of interlocking lightweight tubes, was innovative and successful. Maserati's stiletto-slender Ghibli, designed in the late 1960s by another fabulous Bertone protégé, Giorgetto Giugiaro (who later formed Italdesign), competed closely with Ferrari's 365 GTB/4 Daytona in the early 1970s. Ironically, although they were intense rivals at this time, Ferrari and Maserati both eventually became part of the giant Fiat-Chrysler conglomerate, as did Lancia and Alfa Romeo.

competition from sant'agata bolognese

Ferruccio Lamborghini produced tractors and air conditioners after the war. Having made his fortune with these less glamorous items, Lamborghini elected to develop a grand touring coupe to rival Ferrari's. An oft-repeated tale—that Lamborghini was unhappy with his personal Ferrari and unable to have an audience with Enzo Ferrari about it—is simply not true. Lamborghini had the means and the desire to build his own cars. Franco Scaglione designed the first Lamborghini 350 GTV. Its edgy lines were not universally appreciated, but Felice Bianchi Anderloni at Carrozzeria Touring quickly softened the shape and in 1964 produced the sensational alloy-bodied Lamborghini 350 GT to great initial acclaim (fig. 18).

Lamborghini himself told *Road & Track*'s Athos Evangelisti that he wanted to produce a great GT car, "not a technical bomb."[13] Rivaling Ferrari's 330 GT, the

new Lamborghini had five speeds (compared to four speeds in the Ferrari), independent rear suspension (versus a live axle), four-wheel disc brakes, and a three-hundred-bhp, four-cam V-12 (versus Ferrari's single overhead camshaft [SOHC] engine) designed by Giotto Bizzarrini. The comments of *Il Commendatore* (a popular name for Enzo Ferrari by this point) when he first saw the competition from Lamborghini were not recorded, but he could not have been pleased. *Road & Track*'s Henry Manney III called it "the most desirable sports/GT I have driven."[14]

Ferruccio Lamborghini elected not to spend huge amounts of money racing his cars, and his next effort must have annoyed Ferrari even more. Thanks to the brilliant young engineering team of Gian Paolo Dallara, Paolo Stanzani, and development driver Bob Wallace, the mid-engine Miura was nothing short of sensational. With its four-liter, six-carburetor dual overhead camshaft (DOHC) V-12 mounted transversely behind the driver

and passenger, the impossibly low GT was a more contemporary design than Ferrari's front-engine 365 GTB/4 Daytona and just as fast—and even more so in the improved S and SV variants.

Marcello Gandini (one of Nuccio Bertone's discoveries) designed the Miura. In an interview with Italian car expert Winston Goodfellow, Gandini noted that "the Miura wasn't the creation of a new line. Rather, it was an arrival point of all the sports cars of the 1950s. The lines were very soft, but very animalistic."[15] Gandini would later design the Miura's successor, the outrageous scissor-door Countach LP400 (fig. 19), a car that found a ready market with clients who wanted something a bit different—something a bit more outré than a Ferrari. With these groundbreaking cars, Lamborghini established itself as a world-class contender in the avant-garde luxury market, introducing one outrageous model after another and continuing to the present (now as a division of the Volkswagen Group).

Although Ferrari raced mid-engine sports cars such as the 250 LM (another Le Mans winner), Enzo Ferrari was certain that powerful mid-engine cars for the road were "too dangerous" for his clientele. Sergio Pininfarina, the son of Battista Pininfarina, whose carrozzerie designed most Ferrari road cars, knew that the next important trend would be mid-engine production models. Using a Ferrari 365 P racing chassis, with a 380-hp V-12 engine, Aldo Brovarone, Pininfarina's director of design, working with Sergio Pininfarina, built a design study to rival the Lamborghini Miura. Its unique three-seat design—hence its name "Tre Posti"—featured centralized steering, instruments, and controls, which optimized interior space, provided a high level of visibility, and anticipated the modern McLaren F1 (fig. 20).

Mid-engine berlinettas did not have to have their engines located behind the passenger compartment. Giotto Bizzarrini, who had designed the Ferrari GTO, developed the Corvette-powered Iso Grifo with a front,

midmounted engine, solidifying a trend in which several Italian carmakers such as Argentine racer Alessandro de Tomaso and Milanese industrialist Renzo Rivolta (known as the Bubblecar King and creator of the BMW Isetta) employed big, powerful, and relatively inexpensive Chevrolet and Ford V-8s instead of smaller, more complex, and temperamental Italian-built engines. Frank Reisner's Carrozzeria Intermeccanica built eighty-eight beautiful little Apollo GT roadsters and berlinettas, which were powered by Buick V-8 engines. The Iso Rivolta GT, followed by the Iso Grifo A3/L, proved to be powerful and reliable grand touring cars. They arguably lacked Ferrari's pedigree but were also without a Ferrari's inherent mechanical fussiness.

Bizzarrini and Iso separated in 1965, but Bizzarrini continued on his own, marketing the competition version of the A3/C, the Bizzarrini 5300 Strada (which was also called the 5300 GT America). It was low-slung and sinister, armed with a Corvette V-8 set far back in

its lightweight tubular chassis (giving it a 365+ bhp), and packed a quartet of Weber side-draft carburetors. Built in small numbers in Livorno, the wicked-looking Strada was never a commercial success, but as a thinly disguised, fairly uncompromised race car for the road, it attracted a great deal of positive attention. Bizzarrini said, "I consider it a second-generation 250 GTO."[16]

Italy abounded with small manufacturers (aficionados like to call them "Etceterini"), such as Abarth (fig. 22), Giaur, Moretti, Nardi, Siata, Stanguellini, and others. Many of them used modified Fiat engines and running gear, clothed in lovely Italian coachwork. These Ferraris and Maseratis in miniature found a ready market because they were more affordable than the top-tier marques and they could be raced and rallied successfully.

the battle of the wedges

A number of Italian companies wanted to show just how aerodynamic and utterly low a functioning automobile could become. Nuccio Bertone, who had influenced the design of the BATs for Alfa Romeo, created the startling Alfa Romeo Carabo with Marcello Gandini (fig. 24). The exquisite Carabo, shown in Paris in 1968, was severely wedge-shaped and barely thirty-nine inches high, with gull-wing doors. Not to be outdone, Pininfarina's head of styling, Paolo Martin, presented the Ferrari 512S Modulo (fig. 23) on a Can-Am racing chassis two years later at the Geneva Motor Show (with a design he'd begun in 1967). Featuring a sliding canopy roof that rolls forward for entrance, and partially enclosed wheels, the 36 ¾-inch-high Modulo won countless design awards. The Modulo was not originally a functional vehicle, but noted collector James Glickenhaus purchased the show car from Pininfarina in 2014 and

FIG. 24. 1968 Alfa Romeo Carabo by Bertone

has announced his intention to bring it to an operational state.

Wanting to expand his business (his 308 GT4 for Ferrari was not considered a styling triumph), Nuccio Bertone sought to attract Lancia's attention. Unbeknownst to Lancia management, he bravely combined suspension pieces and an engine from a Lancia Fulvia with a dramatically low wedge-shaped body, eschewing conventional doors in favor of a frontal section that could be raised to allow access and incorporating a steering wheel that would pivot to facilitate driver entry. Bertone drove the 33-inch-high Lancia Stratos HF Zero concept car (fig. 25) to the automaker's headquarters, passing *under* the company barrier to the astonishment of onlookers. While Lancia never built a production Stratos shaped like this one-off car, Bertone was given the assignment to build a radical front-mid-engine Group B rally car, which was also called the Stratos (fig. 26).

on two wheels

After the war, Italian motorcycle manufacturers—Ducati, Gilera, Moto Guzzi, MV Agusta, and others—were quick to match their car-building counterparts, with innovations in engineering and design, powerful and cleverly configured air-cooled engines, and competent race-bred chassis, not to mention countless racing victories. They undoubtedly inspired the fledgling Japanese motorcycle manufacturers and antagonized British manufacturers, and were envied by other European and American companies. Skilled Italian riders such as Giacomo Agostini, who won 122 Grand Prix titles, were yet another reason Italy excelled. This exhibition includes a Ducati V-twin (fig. 27), a four-cylinder MV Agusta, and an unusual eight-cylinder Moto Guzzi, which together dramatize the broad range of Italian motorcycle innovation. Like Italian automobiles, the motorcycles of Italy are perennially exciting

performers, with memorable styling, profound engineering, and the sheer brio that distinguishes them from their rivals.

italy's lasting influence

In 1954, less than a decade after the end of the war, *Road & Track* (America's leading auto publication at the time) commented: "The Italian influence leads the automotive design world. It remains consistent, commanding, spirited and graceful."[17]

Italian cars (and to a lesser extent, motorcycles) from that exciting midcentury period, and cars from other countries with Italian styling and coachwork, had an immense influence on the world of automobiles. Successful racing efforts by Alfa Romeo, Ferrari, Lancia, and Maserati (fig. 28) helped the Italian companies

dominate international competition. Lessons from racing often found their way into the creation of road cars, to the delight of enthusiasts. Today, cars and motorcycles from this period attract very high prices as collector vehicles. They are stunning to look at, are exciting to study, and testify to the imaginative design language that helped generate Italy's industrial renaissance.

1. Quoted in Winston Goodfellow, *Italian Sports Cars* (Osceola, WI: MBI, 2000), 46.

2. Dennis Adler, *The Art of the Sports Car: The Greatest Designs of the 20th Century* (New York: HarperCollins, 2002), 150.

3. To restart his company, Farina coachbuilt an aerodynamic and startlingly different custom cabriolet body, with a long, fashionably flat hood and rounded slab sides, on a 1942 military 6C 2500 Alfa chassis.

4. *8 Automobiles* exhibition catalogue (New York: Museum of Modern Art, 1951), 8.

5. Michel Zumbrunn and Robert Cumberford, *Auto Legends: Classics of Style and Design* (London: Merrell, 2002), 163. Interestingly, the 202's shape was considered so "slippery" that noted hot-rodder and dry lakes racer Bill Burke borrowed a Cisitalia 202 coupe owned by Robert E. Petersen (the Los Angeles publishing magnate who founded *Hot Rod* and *Motor Trend* magazines) and pulled a mold off its curvaceous body to build the first of several fiberglass copies. Burke then raced his Cisitalia wannabe, and a few road-going examples were built; their overhead-valve V-8s made these cars much faster than the four-cylinder originals.

6. Peter Grist, *Virgil Exner, Visioneer* (Dorchester, England: Veloce, 2007).

7. Cunningham tried independently to win the 24 Hours of Le Mans in an American car. Based in West Palm Beach, Florida, he retained a talented team to design and drive his cars. Vignale's proposal for a fastback coupe on Cunningham's rugged tubular chassis echoed some elements of the coachbuilder's creations for Ferrari, on a slightly larger but no less attractive scale.

8. Beverly Rae Kimes, "Over the Top: Boano's Jazzy Lincoln Coupe," *Automobile Quarterly* 41, no. 3 (2001): 33–45.

9. Andrew Nahum, *Fifty Cars That Changed the World* (London: Octopus, 2009), 50.

10. Steve Lehto, *Chrysler's Turbine Car: The Rise and Fall of Detroit's Coolest Creation* (Chicago: Chicago Review Press, 2010), 170–71.

11. Decio Giulio Riccardo Carugati, *Pininfarina: Identity of a Design* (Milan: Electa, 1999), 38.

12. Dean Batchelor, *Illustrated Ferrari Buyer's Guide*, 2nd ed. (Osceola, WI: Motorbooks, 1986), 96.

13. Athos Evangelisti, "Turin Show," *Road & Track*, February 1964, 7.

14. Goodfellow, *Italian Sports Cars*, 79.

15. Ibid., 96.

16. Ibid., 80.

17. "Turin Auto Show," *Road & Track*, August 1954, 18.

FIG. 28. 1972 Maserati Boomerang by
Giorgetto Giugiaro

THE AUTOMOBILES AND MOTORCYCLES

BELLA BERLINETTAS

Cisitalia 202 SC

**THE REVS INSTITUTE FOR AUTOMOTIVE RESEARCH, INC.,
NAPLES, FLORIDA**

If a single design can be said to embody the essence of the Italian automotive renaissance after World War II, it is that of the Cisitalia 202 coupe, of which only 170 examples were built (coupes and derived convertibles combined). The Cisitalia 202 coupe was the first-ever car in the collection of the Museum of Modern Art (MoMA) in New York, and was included in the seminal *8 Automobiles* exhibition at the museum in 1951.

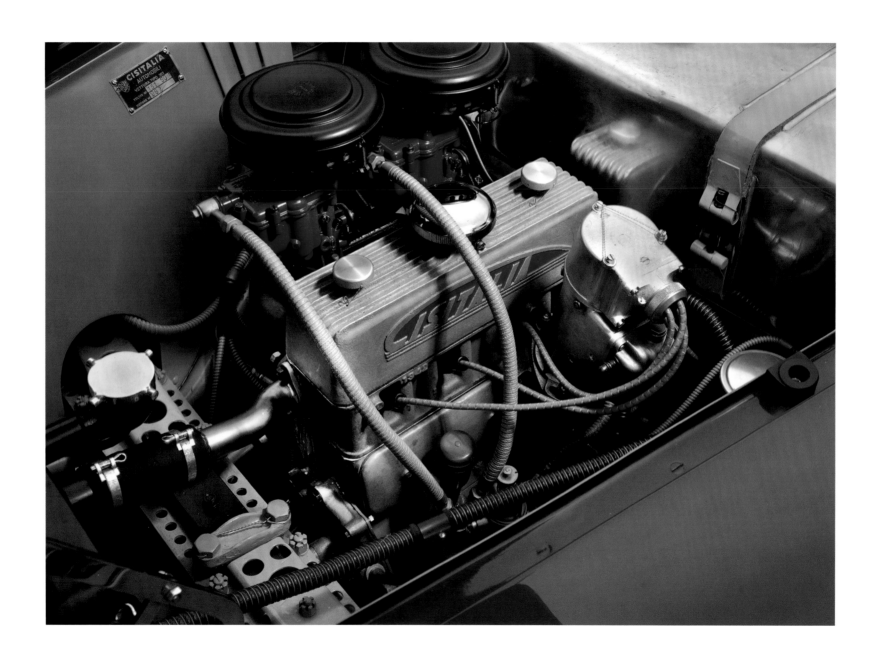

Interestingly, MoMA's first Cisitalia was exchanged for a different example proffered by Pininfarina, the company taking credit for the design, perhaps because the first was one of the copies constructed by carrozzerie Alfredo Vignale and Stabilimenti Farina rather than Pininfarina itself. Regardless of who made their bodies, all 202s used an innovative chassis laid down initially in 1944 by the great Fiat engineer Dante Giacosa—working in his spare time—to the order of Piero Dusio, an ambitious entrepreneur who created the Compagnia Industriale Sportiva Italia (C.I.S. Italia, leading to the more melodious "Cisitalia") to build racing cars.

Giacosa first intended to base road cars on Fiat 500 chassis fitted with Fiat 1100 engines, but as Dusio owned a bicycle factory stocked with steel tubes, Giacosa's imagination shifted to a new tubular chassis that placed driver and engine lower than common practice at the time. As the war wound down and his workload at Fiat increased, Giacosa suggested that Giovanni Savonuzzi, then in Fiat's aircraft engine section, be named Cisitalia's technical director. Taking the post in August 1945, Savonuzzi patented Giacosa's chassis layout on behalf of Cisitalia. The critical February 1947 patent described coachwork "profiled so that the front end is very close to the ground, with the fenders forming two lateral walls that are relatively high in relation to the engine hood." That nicely sums up almost everything following the 202 in car design up to the present day.

The first Cisitalia coupe, nicknamed "the ugly duckling," had a modern centerline profile, but its detailing was definitely pre-1945, with a harp-shaped grille similar to those seen on prewar Mercedes and Alfa Romeo racing cars. Savonuzzi then designed two different open cars: the Razzo, whose body was built by Garella, and the Nuvolari, named after the great Italian driver Tazio Nuvolari. Driving a 202, Nuvolari had finished second in the 1947 Mille Miglia, beaten only at the finish by an Alfa Romeo 8C 2900 (the fastest road car of the 1930s). His feat led to Stabilimenti Farina making a small series of 202 roadsters.

The true progenitor of the revered Pininfarina 202 coupes was made by Carrozzeria Vignale from another Savonuzzi design. It featured the characteristic oval air intake, with multiple vertical bars—bicycle tubes themselves—carrying out the surface that would have existed had no intake opening been cut into the form. From the center of the doors forward, there is almost no difference between the early racing coupes and the car credited entirely—and erroneously—to Pininfarina. The rear of Savonuzzi's coupes—also built by Vignale— was dramatically different, with the roof tapering sharply inward in plain view and the rear fenders topped by huge fins to ensure aerodynamic stability in crosswinds.

Gian Battista "Pinin" (Shorty) Farina was a small man with impeccable taste, a penchant for classicism and simplification, and enormous ambition. To employ a musical metaphor, his design abilities reflect the qualities of a great orchestra conductor more closely than those of a great composer, and as a brilliant synthesis of the ideas of others, the Cisitalia 202 is perhaps the finest expression of his outsize capabilities. The tenth of eleven children, Pinin began working in his brother Giovanni's company at age eleven, a common occurrence more than a hundred years ago. At twenty-seven, he made a trip to the United States with his brother to study American manufacturing methods, an experience vital to his later career as an industrialist. Returning to Italy, Pinin set up his own coachbuilding firm, Carrozzeria Pinin Farina (later Pininfarina), in 1930.

We know now that a single wooden "buck," or reference form, was passed from Pinin Farina to Vignale to Stabilimenti Farina as capacity was available, and that all 202s were built between 1947 and 1949, with the Vignale coupes having an expanded roofline and a slightly taller grille than the others. The rear fender form applied to the side by Pininfarina was much "in the air" at the time, showing up on postwar Studebakers in 1947 and GM's new C bodies in 1948. The result of Pinin's masterly direction was one of the greatest car designs of all time. **RC**

Cunningham C3 Continental

THE REVS INSTITUTE FOR AUTOMOTIVE RESEARCH, INC., NAPLES, FLORIDA

At first glance you might think this sleek berlinetta is a Ferrari. Its racy lines, long hood, and tight cabin whisper "Maranello," but its coachbuilt Vignale body is on a larger scale. And it has quite a history. Briggs S. Cunningham Jr., the famed America's Cup yachtsman, aviator, and auto racer, nearly won the grueling 24 Hours of Le Mans race in the early 1950s, when he developed and fielded a personally financed private racing team that ran a series of Chrysler Hemi V-8-powered sports cars.

Cunningham's goal was to win the French racing classic in an American car, with a US production engine. In 1950 he entered two modified Cadillacs at Le Mans. They finished tenth and eleventh against many of the world's premier, purpose-built sports models.

To enter the next contest with a car bearing his name, he had to be an auto manufacturer. He was required to build twenty-five cars in 1952 and fifty the following year. So Cunningham assembled a talented team of constructors and drivers and set up shop in West Palm Beach, Florida. US automakers at the time didn't consider an American effort at Le Mans to be a priority. When Cadillac wasn't interested, the Cunningham works modified Chrysler's new, soon-to-be-legendary 180-bhp Hemi V-8 to develop 235 bhp, thanks to four Zenith carburetors, improved valve timing, and higher compression. *Mechanix Illustrated*'s Tom McCahill enthused, "Cunningham has reworked the Chrysler so it will match any engine in

the world today."[1] Lacking a suitable Florida track, the Cunningham *equipe* tested its cars at triple-digit speeds on public roads near the factory.

For his Le Mans rematch a year later, a trio of C2 sports cars bore American racing colors (white bodies with twin blue stripes) for the first time. They were loaded aboard the France-bound SS *Mauretania*. Powerful, but too heavy and plagued by low-octane French fuel, the C2s still showed promise. One car held second place for six hours and topped 152 mph on the Mulsanne straight but ultimately failed to win.

As he developed his next race cars, Cunningham also turned his attention to a GT model. The new production models, called C3s, would satisfy the manufacturing requirements of the French authorities and help to finance Cunningham's expensive racing operation. Cunningham and his small team, led by Phil Walters and Briggs Weaver, developed both coupes and convertibles.

To save money, the C3's rugged, tubular, cruciform-braced chassis was assembled in Florida and then shipped to Turin, Italy, where attractive alloy bodies designed by Giovanni Michelotti were fabricated and installed by Carrozzeria Vignale. The cars were then returned to West Palm Beach, where they were inspected, tested for two hundred miles (an unprecedented distance—no other manufacturer did this much testing on each new car), and detailed. Vignale was a respected coachbuilder whose elegant designs had appeared on Ferrari and Maserati chassis. Michelotti succumbed to the early 1950s styling gimmick of a false hood scoop, but the C3's flush-fitted, flip-out door handles were a lovely Italian touch, and the car's deeply sculpted body sides provided a natural break for two-tone paint schemes, which helped make the car appear thinner and more svelte. The design gave Cunningham overnight credibility, although the trans-oceanic build process was unnecessarily expensive.

In 1953 Arthur Drexler, curator of architecture at the Museum of Modern Art in New York, named the Cunningham C3 one of the "10 Best Contemporary Automobiles." The only other American car chosen was Raymond Loewy's Studebaker Starliner. Sold new in 1953, this C3 was bought by a California man and then changed hands several times. It was road tested by *Road & Track*'s editor, John Bond, and then repurchased by Briggs Cunningham for personal transportation. A plaque on the dash reads "0–60, 6.2 sec; 0–100, 15.4 sec."

Cunningham's Italian-American C3s were big, powerful, and very fast. If they had been fighter planes, they would have been Republic P-47 Thunderbolts, not sleek North American P-51 Mustangs. With their basso profundo, thundering V-8s sounded very different from the high-pitched V-12s in the Ferraris. The Chrysler Hemi V-8, named for its hemisphere-shaped combustion chambers, was the most powerful production engine available—a large-displacement brute capable of long hours at top revs. Not to mention the lovely Italian coachwork. Sadly, at a then-pricey $10,000–$12,000, they never caught on. Total production was only eighteen coupes and nine convertibles. After five years of red ink mixed with racing fuel, Cunningham retired his manufacturing operation and became Jaguar's racing representative in North America.

I was just a kid in 1955 when Cunningham caught my attention: here was this tiny independent American carmaker who took on the world's best and came close to winning Le Mans. In 1951, Cunningham was running second overall in the Sarthe Classic before a mechanical failure took him out of contention. In 1952, Cunningham finished fourth overall at Le Mans in a C4-R, and in 1953, a C5-R won its class and finished third overall. In 1956, a C6-R unfortunately had to be retired early, and that was the last year Briggs raced at Le Mans in one of his own cars. At that time, Chevrolet Corvettes and Ford Thunderbirds were simply boulevard cruisers. The Cunningham was the real thing. Its presence on the market was short lived, but the existing cars are highly respected and valuable today. The Cunningham C3 is a reminder of one man's dedication and his artist's eye for detail. **KG**

1. Ken Gross, "Born to Run, 1954 Cunningham C-3 Cabriolet," *Special Interest Autos*, April 1984, 13.

Fiat 8V Supersonic

COLLECTION OF PAUL GOULD, PATTERSON, NEW YORK

Although this Fiat and all but the very first of the various Supersonic bodies—on Alfa Romeo, Aston Martin, Fiat, and Jaguar chassis—were made by Carrozzeria Ghia, the original design was created by Giovanni Savonuzzi, years before he became head of engineering for the Torinese coachbuilder. It was a one-off design done for a friend, Virgilio Conrero, who was then building a reputation as a "tuner" (the polite European term for what Americans call a hot-rodder) of Alfa Romeo 1900s. The prototype body to this highly dramatic design was made by Alfredo Vignale, who had built bodies for Savonuzzi's Cisitalia racers in 1947.

Savonuzzi not only designed the chassis frame and suspension tweaks for the Alfa components Conrero used, he also came up with this startling shape, its headlamps leading the way like the business end of a guided missile. Applying what he had learned from using the small wind tunnel at the Politecnico di Torino, where he earned his engineering degree, and from his experiences with Cisitalia racing cars, Savonuzzi achieved an on-the-road drag coefficient lower than the best car in production anywhere in the world in 1952, Porsche's 356 coupe. That figure was verified by tests on a Fiat-based Supersonic like this one in the advanced Pininfarina wind tunnel more than half a century after the cars were built. The designer's instincts and intuition were more than enough compensation for the relatively feeble technical means available in the early 1950s in Italy.

Fiat built only 114 8V examples. All but one were steel-bodied coupes. The nomenclature derived from the fact that Fiat's directors erroneously believed that Ford Motor Company had patented the name "V-8." In its most powerful form, the 8V two-liter engine developed a creditable 127 bhp, and the performance of the sturdy Fiat-built cars was not impressive, with a top speed of only 105 mph. But Fiat sold about one hundred additional bare chassis carrying its unusual narrow-angle (70-degree) V-8 engine to Turin-based sports car specialist Siata and others to several coachbuilders, Ghia among them.

The Supersonics were faster than the Fiats, of course, but they were not really competition cars, as they were too big and heavy for serious racing. That did not prevent some of them from running in the classical Mille Miglia races, where they accounted for themselves nicely, although Conrero's prototype, the first vehicle to bear the wonderfully apt and provocative Supersonic name, crashed and burned in its only attempt. The Fiat chassis and Ghia bodies were strong enough to allow

considerable liberties to be taken. General Motors' interior design chief Henry de Segur Lauve had a 4.3-liter Chevrolet small-block V-8 installed in his Supersonic in 1956, and Willment Engineering in the United Kingdom fitted a seven-liter Ford V-8 to one in the mid-1960s.

The car was influential in styling, too. The "booms" on the sides of 1958 Chevrolets were copied directly from Lauve's car, and the tight, elegant upper cabin, with its outstanding visibility, was adapted to the Volkswagen Karmann Ghia coupes in the 1950s, a surprising collaboration between Savonuzzi, by then chief designer at Ghia, and Virgil Exner, Chrysler's design chief. Chrysler had worked with Ghia since 1950. Its first publicly announced concept car, the K-310 two-seat coupe, led to a series of show cars and specialty models such as the Dual-Ghia cars (Ghia-built with Dodge chassis) beloved of the Hollywood "Rat Pack" led by Frank Sinatra. All the members—Joey Bishop, Sammy Davis Jr., Peter Lawford, and Dean Martin—drove Ghia-bodied Chrysler-based cars. Although the Supersonic design would have been perfect for American chassis, Ghia had moved on, and those examples built on Italian and British platforms remain the heart of the program. Proof that the Supersonics were good, well-built cars can be seen in the fact that this particular Supersonic was kept—and used—by its original owner for fifty-five years. It was auctioned for $1.76 million not long ago.

As befits cars that were essentially handmade, there are variations from the base design on each example. There are summary bumpers on some cars, and some have hood scoops. But all are beautiful, efficient, and worthy of the preservation they have enjoyed, and they stand as evidence of the exceptional talents of Giovanni Savonuzzi, perhaps the most important but least known of the Italian designers who led the world in automobile design from 1945 to 1975. **RC**

Alfa Romeo BAT 5, BAT 7 & BAT 9

THE BLACKHAWK COLLECTION, DANVILLE, CALIFORNIA

The grand renaissance of automotive styling began in Italy in the late 1940s, with cars such as Pininfarina's lovely Cisitalia 202 coupe and the Maserati A6 1500. Barely a decade later, Carrozzeria Bertone in Milan was responsible for three of the most memorable concept cars ever conceived. Giuseppe "Nuccio" Bertone and his talented chief designer, former aeronautics student and women's fashion designer Franco Scaglione, were intrigued with the possibility of creating a series of visually stunning, aerodynamically efficient sports coupes with the lowest possible coefficient of drag (Cd).

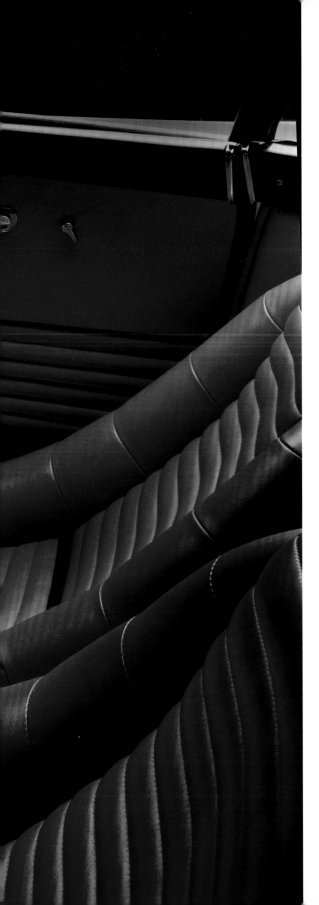

The resulting cars used the sporting Alfa Romeo 1900 chassis and were strongly influenced by the newly emerging jet aircraft industry. They were aptly named BATs, using the initials for "Berlinetta Aerodinamica Tecnica." The "BAT" name, as it was popularly written, was just perfect because the cars' imaginative tail fin treatments were reminiscent of stylized bat wings. Alfa authority Joe Benson adds, "The BAT acronym was so appropriate that it couldn't have been accidental."[1]

The BAT 5 was the first to break cover, at the 1953 Turin Auto Show. To achieve its radically low Cd, and to eliminate as many air vortices as possible, the designers of the BAT 5's curvaceous aluminum body bestowed on it a smoothly protruding round nose section, flanked by two large air openings that closely resembled paired jet air intakes. The front and rear wheels were almost completely enclosed, which reduced the resistance created by the turning wheels. Winston Goodfellow called Scaglione "an artist with sheet metal."[2] Certainly the BAT series proves his point.

The BAT 5's low and wide panoramic wraparound windscreen and slanted side windows (raked at a steep 45-degree angle) were joined to a virtually flat roof, which seamlessly tapered into a split rear window with a slender divider that separated a pair of elegant fins. The BAT 5's 75-hp twin-cam engine, its light overall weight (2,400 pounds), and the car's near-perfect aerodynamics—its Cd was a then-impressive 0.23—permitted a 200-kph (120-mph) top speed, reportedly with excellent stability at high speeds.

Design and technology expert Andrew Nahum called the BAT 5 "the sensation of the 1953 Salone dell'automobile di Torino," adding that "it was more than a sensational catchpenny glamour exercise—it had 38 percent less drag than the 'donor' car, meaning that a 50 percent larger engine would have been needed to give the standard Alfa Romeo the same performance."[3]

The BAT 5 attracted an immense amount of interest for Bertone and Scaglione, but Alfa Romeo had no plans for a limited-production version of this show car.

It would have been very hard to build, and likely too expensive, given the 1900 model's already high price point. But Carrozzeria Bertone's work had just begun. Another brilliant BAT would soon soar from where its predecessor began.

Introduced at the 1954 Turin show, the BAT 7's design built on BAT 5's almost shocking styling cues. Bertone and Scaglione had closely studied aircraft wing profiles, which resulted in more dramatically curved, even longer tail fins for their newest show car. Scaglione lowered the BAT 7's nose and reworked the flanking air intakes for still more aerodynamic efficiency. The center spine arched like a finned flying buttress before smoothly joining the rounded tail section. Many people consider the BAT 7 to be the most dramatic example of the wild Bertone trio. The changes to the original design reduced the Cd to just 0.19, which would prove to be the lowest number achieved by any of the three prototypes.

Writer Serge Bellu noted, "A true 'dream car' in the sense in which this was meant in the 1950s, BAT 7 swung between lyricism and naiveté, with its frankly simplistic detailing borrowed from the world of aviation, its over-the-top fins, and its air intakes suggesting the power of a jet engine. Thanks to the talent of Franco Scaglione, the language became poetic, the scrolls of the rear contracting as if they were the wings of a frightened bird."[4]

The third car in this still-celebrated midcentury trio of Bertone coupes was the BAT 9. With this iteration, an attempt was made to eliminate some of the earlier cars' more exaggerated styling elements, and to integrate a few contemporary Alfa Romeo design cues. For the BAT 9, the air intakes were reduced in size, an almost conventional-looking Alfa vertical grille was used, and the tail fins were smaller and more angular than the dramatic and curvaceous appendages on the first two BATs. But the car is still a knockout, suggesting that had Alfa Romeo elected to duplicate it for production—which they never did—this design exercise could have been practical. Noted designer and critic Robert Cumberford called the BATs "astonishing" and wrote that "with their extreme tail fins, rounded windscreens and extremely low drag coefficients, they were beyond style."[5]

Franco Scaglione had served five years as a prisoner of war before beginning his postwar civilian career. Goodfellow called him "perhaps the most mercurial figure in Italy's styling world."[6] Cumberford wrote that Scaglione was "very possibly the greatest of many designers 'discovered' and nurtured by Bertone."[7] Bertone went on to mentor Giorgetto Giugiaro and Marcello Gandini. Nahum wrote that "these three outstanding designers made Bertone, for a while, the centre of maximum imagination for the development of the postwar car, and their selection is a tribute to the judgment of proprietor Giuseppe 'Nuccio' Bertone."[8]

Instead of producing the BAT 9, Bertone created the limited-edition Sprint Speciale series for Alfa Romeo, from 1957 to 1962, using styling cues from all three BAT prototypes. The Sprint Speciales also borrowed design elements from Alfa Romeo's famed Disco Volante (Flying Saucer) race cars of the early 1950s. Thanks to its refined aerodynamics, acquired from the BAT experiments, the production Sprint Speciale could top 124 mph with a relatively small, 1,300 cc (cubic centimeters) Alfa Giulietta engine.

In 2008, in Geneva (but not at the Geneva Motor Show), Carrozzeria Bertone presented a modern successor to the 1950s series. Based on a new Alfa Romeo 8C Competizione chassis, the new BAT 11 displayed many of the early show cars' design elements, but this show car was more angular than softly rounded, and executed in a thoroughly modern form. Arguably far less attractive than its trio of forebears, it proved to be a one-of-a-kind exercise and was not put into production.

The original three BAT 5-7-9 concept cars are still very exciting to see. While journalist and professor Larry Edsall wryly commented that the BAT analogy "took the motorcar into a frightening fictional universe," he praised their creator, saying, "With the B.A.T.s, Bertone joined the aristocracy of the styling world."[9] **KG**

1. Joe Benson, *The Illustrated Alfa Romeo Buyer's Guide* (Osceola, WI: Motorbooks, 1983), 160.

2. Winston Goodfellow, *Italian Sports Cars* (Osceola, WI: MBI, 2000), 53.

3. Andrew Nahum, *Fifty Cars That Changed the World* (London: Octopus, 2009), 46.

4. Serge Bellu, *500 Fantastic Cars* (Paris: Editions Solar, 2002), 27.

5. Michel Zumbrunn and Robert Cumberford, *Auto Legends: Classics of Style and Design* (London: Merrell, 2004), 280–81.

6. Goodfellow, *Italian Sports Cars*, 53.

7. Zumbrunn and Cumberford, *Auto Legends*, 280–81.

8. Nahum, *Fifty Cars*, 46–47.

9. Larry Edsall, *Concept Cars: From the 1930s to the Present* (New York: Fall River Press, 2009), 49–50.

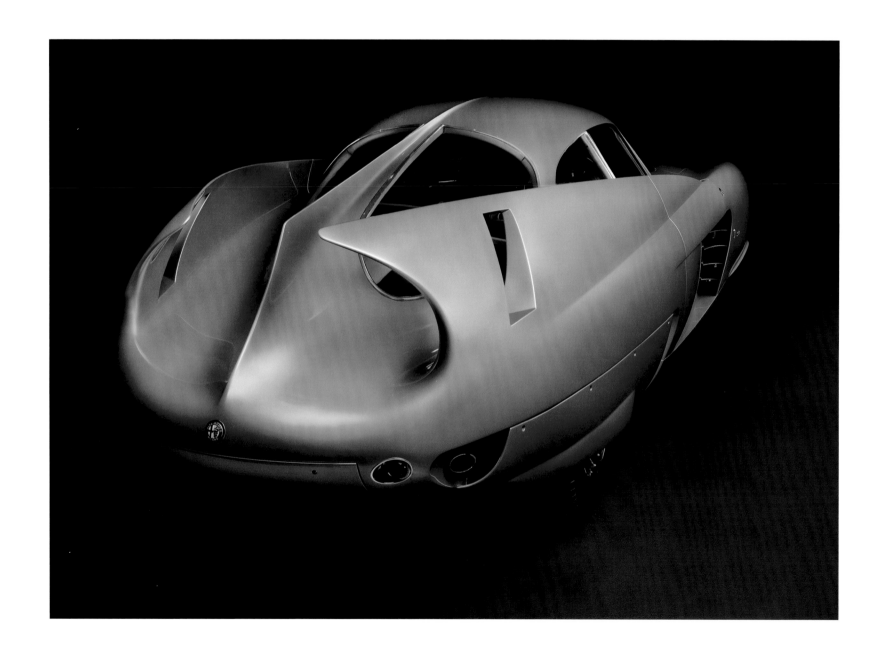

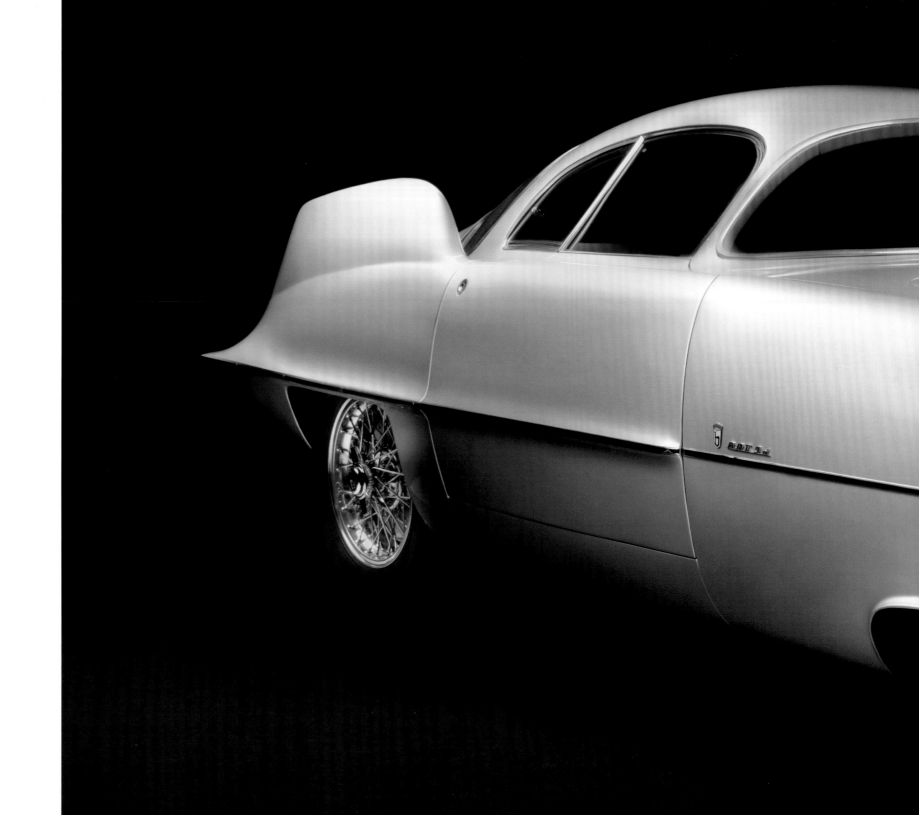

Ferrari 250 GTO

COLLECTION OF BERNARD AND JOAN CARL, WASHINGTON, D.C.

The Ferrari 250 GTO is an extraordinary automobile. Its performance and history are legendary, it's truly a beautiful—no, make that gorgeous—sculptural object, and at $50 million for one at a recent sale, it's the most expensive car ever sold to a private buyer. The story of Automobili Ferrari's claim that it was a regular production model, reinforced by the ostentatious Gran Turismo Omologato (Grand Touring Homologated) name, is almost as legendary as the car itself.

Omologato, derived from ancient Greek, is the modern Italian word for the process of registering a product with the relevant authorities, in this case with the FIA (Fédération Internationale de l'Automobile) world sporting group. Some thirty-three Series I GTOs were made by Ferrari, and three Series IIs were produced along with three four-liter versions, so the total is just thirty-nine examples. That it mattered at all is because fifty identical cars had to have been made—and sold—to allow participation in world championship racing events, and Enzo Ferrari desperately wanted to be a world champion constructor.

The mechanical setup was straightforward. Engineer Giotto Bizzarrini laid out the chassis as a variation of the 250 SWB (short wheelbase) model, but installed the three-liter, six-carburetor engine of the Testa Rossa sports racer and a five-speed gearbox. The V-12 was mounted lower and farther back in the chassis for a lower center of gravity and more neutral handling characteristics. The resultant GTO was lighter, and with its reshaped front end and other refinements, it was more aerodynamic than the SWB.[1] Ferrari claimed that this much more focused, racing-oriented chassis was really just the same as that of the earlier semiluxurious grand touring car. When that was challenged, Ferrari threatened to withdraw from racing altogether, which would have distressed fans all over Europe, and indeed all over the world.

The FIA subsequently yielded and allowed GTOs to race. The first event was the 12 Hours of Sebring, in Florida, where American Formula 1 world champion Phil Hill was assigned to drive this very GTO, S/N (serial number) 3387 GT, with Olivier Gendebien, with whom he twice won the 24 Heures du Mans. Both drivers were seriously annoyed at being relegated to the GT category, but the car was so fast in a straight line that they ultimately finished second overall—not far behind the winners, who were in a Ferrari TRI/61, at that. Not long afterward, this car finished sixth overall at Le Mans and third in the GT class. It had a distinguished racing career for four years.

Even the transcendent body design that has been so admired is not quite as series-production as Ferrari would like the world to think. It was not created by the hallowed house of Pininfarina that designed most Ferrari road cars, nor was it shaped by Sergio Scaglietti, who founded the eponymous Carrozzeria Scaglietti and built most Ferrari racer bodies before ceding ownership to Ferrari. The not-fifty-unit series was indeed built in Modena in Scaglietti's shops, but the shape itself was from the inspired hands and eyes of Gian Carlo Guerra, a modest panel-beating workman who had one day said simply, "I know what to do." And he did, bending up a skeletal outline of what he wanted to see with aluminum wires, and then hammering sheets of metal to fit the

contours he'd sketched in three dimensions to achieve those perfect proportions. Enzo Ferrari himself approved it for production. Guerra, the not-often-recognized designer of that Ferrari masterpiece, also wire-framed and built the slightly later and very lovely 275 GTB.

There was a lot of turmoil and ferment at Ferrari at the beginning of the 1960s, and Bizzarrini left Ferrari, along with many others.[2] The GTO was fine-tuned by Mauro Forghieri, a newly hired young engineer who later ran the Formula 1 Scuderia, and by Sergio Scaglietti, the wise old hand. Its superb aerodynamics were perfected by extensive testing. Even though it did not come into existence through normal channels, it is reasonable to say that the GTO was and is the ultimate expression of the classical front-engine racing sports car. And, as is evident from the astonishing prices attained by GTOs today, it is also the most desirable of all sports cars ever made. **RC**

1. Glen Smale, *Ferrari 250 GTO Owner's Workshop Manual* (Somerset, England: Haynes, 2014), 16–17.

2. See Gross's introduction and Goodfellow's essay on the ATS 2500 in this volume for two accounts of the mass departure.

AUTO SHOW STARS

Lancia B52 Aurelia PF200 Spider

COLLECTION OF LINDA AND BILL POPE, PARADISE VALLEY, ARIZONA

Lancia is a marque that's not well known to many Americans, but the firm has produced remarkable road and racing cars. From his company's inception in 1906, Vincenzo Lancia offered technically advanced models, with pioneering features such as sliding pillar independent front suspensions (combining the spring and hydraulic shock absorber in one unit), five-speed transaxles, monocoque bodies, narrow-angle V-6 and later V-4 engines, and much more. Lancias were sporty, high-performance cars, with the perfect chassis dimensions to attract custom coachwork.

After Pinin Farina's stylishly successful efforts on the Cisitalia 202, many wealthy cognoscenti requested the carrozzeria's design work on other marques. Lancia's sporty Aurelia coupe, introduced in 1951, had an advanced unit body, albeit a rather plain design, but the rest of the specification was very exciting: a two-liter twin-cam, dual-carburetor V-6, independent front and rear suspensions, and race-inspired inboard drum brakes. It was a perfect sporting platform, just begging for an exciting body design. For the 1952 Turin Auto Show, to demonstrate his firm's creativity, Pinin Farina presented an imaginative concept car on the Lancia B52 Aurelia chassis.

Just fifty-two Lancia B52s were produced, and they all carried bespoke or limited-production coachwork. Their inspiration came from the skies. By the early 1950s, after the dramatic breaking of the sound barrier in the United States, jet aircraft and rockets were a major design inspiration for Italy's custom body build-ers. Pinin Farina's Lancia PF200, one of a series of just three open cars and three (possibly four) coupes, was a stunner. In the front, a large oval grille opening, ringed with a wide chromed bezel, resembled the yawning air intake on a North American F-86 Sabre jet, the preeminent supersonic US fighter aircraft of that era. Tiny bumperettes and a discrete hood scoop were additional complementary features.

The PF200's trim fuselage curved rearward with long sweeping lines that flowed into a tapered tail, flanked by discrete fins. Fully radiused wheel openings, a raked, slightly curved windscreen with slender pillars, and a trio of small decorative side strakes on a few of the cars were contemporary touches that lent the dashing spider a look of continued movement, even when it was stand-ing still. Each of the Pinin Farina PF200 coupes differed slightly from one another, as did the open versions. Exquisite details such as chromed triple hash mark side trim, through-the-bumper exhausts—six of them—and even a raised windscreen element on the drivers' side were some of the differentiating features.

These lovely Lancia spiders and coupes were a harbinger of great things to come from Battista Pinin Farina. That he was imbued with a special sense of style and design was evident from the beginning. He later wrote in his memoirs that "in the mountains I used to see how the wind sculpted the snow at the edges of the road, digging out different shapes, curved in some places and sharp where it was broken. . . . I wanted to 'copy' those lines for my designs." Farina would reflect that "I was aiming for essentiality. What you take off counts more than what you add on."[1]

Although simplicity and purity of line were always Pinin Farina hallmarks, the military jet aircraft–inspired coachwork on this spider was not carried over into production Lancia Aurelias. Perhaps it was too avant-garde? Also, perhaps because the stylists were trying many approaches, the closed cars and open variants differed considerably from one another. Production Aurelias are very desirable collector cars today, and the special PF200s have become seven-figure stars.

The Lancia B52 Spider was built in extremely limited numbers; it was joined later in 1952 by a berlinetta version. But the coupe wasn't the last Pinin Farina design to use the jet-inspired design. In 1954 Pinin and his craftsmen made a one-off Cadillac 62 Cabriolet Speciale for jazzman Norman Granz that could have easily passed for this Lancia's larger American cousin. Elements of this design were also used as part of Carrozzeria Pinin Farina's styling work for Nash in 1956, when the firm built the saucy Rambler Palm Beach Special concept car. **WG/KG**

1. Quoted in Ernesto Caballo, *Pininfarina: Born with the Automobile* (Milan, Italy: Automobilia, 1993), 74.

1955

Chrysler
Ghia Gilda

COLLECTION OF KATHLEEN REDMOND AND SCOTT GRUNDFOR,
ARROYO GRANDE, CALIFORNIA

In the exuberant post–World War II era, automobile design was heavily influenced by jet aircraft styling. Cadillac's tail fins appeared in 1948. Other makes soon followed, and by the mid-1950s, sharply pointed appendages on automobile rear fenders were ubiquitous. Chrysler's renowned styling chief, Virgil Exner, was determined to prove that aero design wasn't risky in the marketplace—that, after the devastating war years, consumers were eager to embrace the design cues of the future—and that fins could be functional on cars.

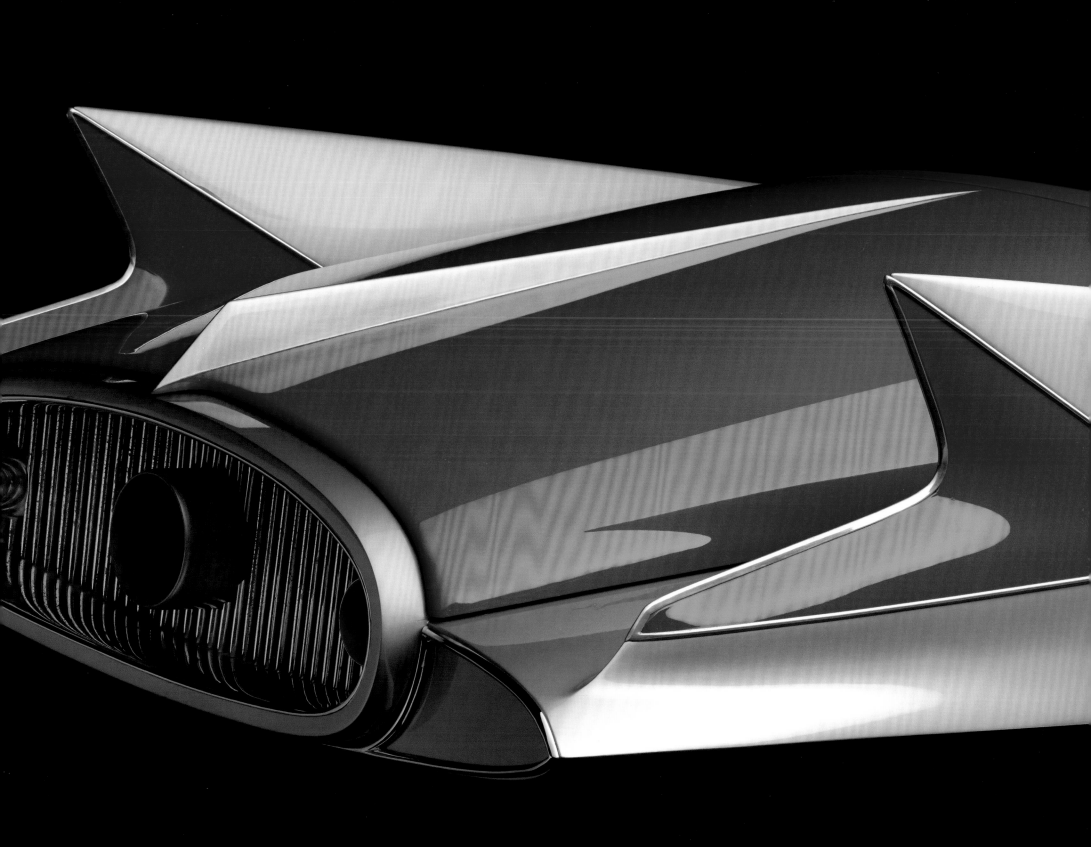

Exner directed Carrozzeria Ghia's designers, under Luigi Segre, to produce a plan for a wedge-shaped coupe. They built a one-half-scale model with fins that could be altered and measured progressively during wind tunnel testing at the Politecnico di Torino. Giovanni Savonuzzi, Ghia's brilliant technical director, concluded that tapered tail fins improved the model's directional stability in crosswinds at high speeds.[1] Then, for the 1955 Salone dell'automobile di Torino, Ghia built a full-scale mockup with an interior but no engine, and called it the Gilda, after the 1946 film noir starring Hollywood actress Rita Hayworth.

Savonuzzi's daughter Alberta told Winston Goodfellow that her father had been influenced by an ad for the movie. It called Hayworth a "super-sexy bomb," and "when he read that description, the name Gilda

stuck with him. He couldn't resist calling the car that."[2] Painted a startling pairing of silver and orange, with arrow-shaped door handles that accentuated the show car's slippery silhouette, the Gilda was a big hit in Turin, where it was presented as "shaped by the wind."[3]

Originally, the show car was to have been fitted with a 1,500 cc OSCA (Officine Specializzate Costruzione Automobili) four-cylinder gasoline engine, which in theory would have permitted a top speed of 140 mph. In *Motor Trend*'s September 1955 issue, there was speculation about whether the "X" in "The Engine-less Ghia X" stood for Chrysler's gas turbine (that is, the engine to be put into the Gilda). But the car never reached that stage of production. Instead, Savonuzzi went to Chrysler in 1956 and played a significant role in developing Chrysler's 1963 Turbine Car.[4]

Exner then ordered a running four-passenger, two-door prototype called the Dart, to be built on a 129-inch-wheelbase Imperial chassis, using information learned from the Gilda exercise. It was tested for more than one hundred thousand miles with a companion four-door model. The two prototypes validated a position paper that Exner presented in 1957, which claimed legitimate advantages for fins as aerodynamic aids on passenger car bodies, earning respect for Chrysler for what had become a popular styling trend. The Gilda show car inspired the futuristic Dart and influenced Chrysler's entire 1957 "Forward Look" styling theme.[5]

After its career as a show car ended, the Ghia Gilda prototype was displayed at the Henry Ford Museum until 1969. It was then at the famed Harrah Collection in Reno, and subsequently at the Blackhawk Collection

in Danville, California, along with other Ghia show cars. Scott Grundfor, a highly respected Mercedes-Benz restorer, purchased the Gilda more than twenty years ago, in excellent, unrestored condition. Grundfor had the skill and wherewithal to install a gas turbine power plant, a development he feels could have happened when the Gilda was first designed. He bought a period-correct, AiResearch single-stage turbine, power transfer case, and Hydrostatic automatic gearbox. These components were installed in such a way that the integrity of the original model was maintained, and they can be easily removed.

For a low-slung, edgy car that looks for all the world like a wingless jet aircraft, the Gilda's powerful gas turbine power plant, with its characteristically shrill jet engine whine, is the perfect complement. Now nearly sixty years old, but far ahead of its time, the stunning Ghia Gilda still attracts appreciative spectators who think it's a much younger car. The Gilda has inspired many famous designers, including the former head of Mercedes-Benz styling, Bruno Sacco, and the late Strother MacMinn, one of America's most influential designers and teachers, who called it "one of the 10 most significant showcars ever built."[6] **KG**

1. John Lamm and the staff of *Road & Track*, *Show Cars* (Newport Beach, CA: CBS Magazines, 1984), 58.

2. Winston Goodfellow, "Ghia's Gilda," *Motor Trend Classic*, Fall 2012, 64–71.

3. Quoted in Jessica Donaldson, "1955 Ghia Gilda Concept," *Conceptcarz* (accessed September 15, 2015), www.conceptcarz.com/vehicle/z5599/Ghia-Gilda-Concept.aspx.

4. Ibid.

5. Peter Grist, *Virgil Exner, Visioneer* (Dorchester, England: Veloce, 2007), 98–101.

6. Goodfellow, "Ghia's Gilda," 70.

1955
Lincoln Indianapolis

COLLECTION OF JAMES E. PETERSEN JR., HOUSTON, TEXAS

In the mid-1950s, Cadillac, Imperial, Lincoln, and Packard vied for America's lucrative luxury car business. Cadillac owned the styling and sales crowns, Imperial was a stylish fringe player, Packard clung to waning prestige, and Lincoln, fresh from 1-2-3 victories in La Carrera Panamericana (The Mexican Road Race), built cars with predictable styling. Dream cars such as the Cadillac El Camino, Chrysler Falcon, and Packard Predicta hinted at where those firms might go in the future.

Not to be outdone, Lincoln showed its twin-canopy, fin-bedecked Futura concept, but it was too avant-garde for production.

As I discussed in the introduction to this catalogue, Italian carrozzerie lusted after the possibilities posed by the American market after World War II. Felice Mario Boano's streamlined styling exercise on a Lincoln chassis attracted attention at the Salone di Torino in 1955. The luscious orange Italian-bodied luxury coupe had *Auto Age* magazine's editors wondering out loud, "Is this the next Lincoln?"[1]

Boano was a mild-mannered, talented stylist with proven management ability. As Giacinto Ghia lay dying, midway through World War II, he asked his wife to enlist Boano to preserve his company. Before the war, Boano had been a designer with Stabilimenti Farina, followed by a stint with Battista Pinin Farina. He then worked for four years as a subcontractor before returning to Carrozzeria Pinin Farina. He was known as "the magician of the auto bodies."[2] After the war, he served as Ghia's chief designer, and then as the firm's co-owner and managing director.

He excelled at adapting the design work of others to full-scale production. At Ghia, working with the clever but temperamental Luigi Segre and using Franco Scaglione's concept drawings, Boano accomplished that task with the acclaimed Alfa Romeo Giulietta Sprint, and he later designed an attractive grand touring (GT) sports coupe on the sporting Lancia Aurelia platform that became the classic Lancia B20 fastback.

Eventually forced out of Ghia by an aggressive and abusive Luigi Segre (Boano wanted to concentrate on the Italian market; Segre wanted to work for American

carmakers), he established Carrozzeria Boano in 1953 with a partner, Luciano Pollo. The elder Boano was assisted by his son, Gian Paolo, who added a youthful design perspective to his father's more traditional approach; Gian Paolo was twenty-four years old when a mysterious insider named John Cuccio at Ford Motor Company offered to introduce the Boanos' work to key decision makers in Dearborn.

A new Lincoln chassis was procured and Gian Paolo began crafting a prototype for the 1955 Turin show. The younger Boano told historian Beverly Rae Kimes that his inspiration was a photo of an Indy 500 pace car, which his father had brought back from a trip to the United States.[3] Gian Paolo's design for the Indianapolis was also influenced by jet aircraft. Carrozzeria Boano's craftsmen worked a tubular frame and yards of sheet metal into a dramatic shape that owed little to previous Lincoln styling efforts. The resulting coupe boasted a very long hood, which extended downward to a vestigial front bumper and thence to an essentially grille-less "bottom-breather" air intake. This car's prominent front fenders and quad headlamps swept rearward into large vertical air scoops that defined the leading edge of the rear fenders. A panoramic windshield, a popular styling cliché of that era, fronted a taut low-roofed cabin with a wraparound rear window. The instruments were hidden under a centrally located folding panel.

The scheme to attract American attention succeeded, as Ford offered the Boanos a ten-year contract—but Mario Boano reported this development to Fiat and subsequently agreed to instead establish Centro Stile, Fiat's in-house styling department. The Indianapolis was doomed from the outset. Lincoln was simultaneously

developing the Continental Mark II and had no need for another personal coupe. Despite its name, the Indianapolis was more boulevard cruiser than sports car, even though the side badging with a checkered-flag motif, a black-and-white checkered interior, wire wheels, and bold flame-orange paint all hinted at a competition car. Henry Ford II took possession of the Indianapolis for a time, and some believe he later gave it to Hollywood heartthrob Errol Flynn.

Whatever its history with Flynn may be, the Indianapolis passed through several owners after the actor's death. It suffered an interior fire and then was partially disassembled and stored for decades. Restorer Jim Cox found redoing the Indianapolis to be a challenge, because it was a one-off to begin with, had been built hastily to meet the Turin show deadline, and was never conceived as an operational road-going car. Original photos of the Indianapolis at Turin helped ensure restoration accuracy. Following its rebirth, Boano's masterpiece won top awards at several concours, including the event at Pebble Beach. Kimes concluded, "The unique interpretation that Gian Paolo gave to an American idiom, the quintessence of the '50s that is the Indianapolis, represents one part of the car's heritage. The other is history itself."[4] **KG**

1. *Auto Age* (cover), November 1955.
2. Beverly Rae Kimes, "Over the Top: Boano's Jazzy Lincoln Coupe," *Automobile Quarterly* 41, no. 3 (Third Quarter 2001): 35.
3. Ibid., 37.
4. Ibid., 43.

Ferrari 400 Superamerica Pininfarina Series II Aerodinamico

COLLECTION OF BERNARD AND JOAN CARL, WASHINGTON, D.C.

Enzo Ferrari grasped the essence of what wealthy Americans wanted in a luxury car—big cars with big engines—well before any of his European contemporaries. At a time when most European manufacturers built engines smaller than 2.8 liters (to avoid the punitive displacement-based taxation European countries crafted to protect their home industries by hindering sales of the 2.9-liter Model T Ford), Ferrari brought out a 4.1-liter V-12 sports car in 1950, unambiguously naming it the Ferrari America.

It had the second basic Ferrari V-12 engine architecture laid out by Aurelio Lampredi. Focused on racing applications, it is commonly called the long-block engine, and it was used in the Formula 1 Ferraris that put an end to Alfa Romeo's long domination of F1 racing.

Making only a very few ultrahigh-performance luxury GT cars each year turned out to be a great way for Ferrari to enhance both its reputation and its profits, and the big-engine America, Superamerica, and Superfast series with varying model numbers, displacements, and power levels were highly successful. But not even a company such as Ferrari is immune to the desire to reduce costs while increasing prices, so it was decided to make some exclusive 400 Superamericas with the cheaper-to-build small-block Colombo engine that began with the 1,500 cc 125S V-12 in 1947 and then developed as the principal Ferrari road car power plant for decades. So far as customers were concerned, *any* Ferrari V-12 was more than acceptable when compared to anything else available.

Ferrari did not manufacture many of these big-engine, big-price-tag cars; a total of forty-seven were built, with this example being the twenty-eighth. Each 400 SA was at least slightly different in color, trim, accessories, and body details from the others. Some have driving lights in the grille. A few have covered headlights. Some have full fender skirts, which allowed knock-off wheel nut exposure while at the same time permitting the body crease line to run from the front wheel opening to the rear bumper tip. To my eye, this iteration is preferable: the grille remains a classical pure oval unencumbered by lamps, and the full rear wheel opening emphasizes the enormous power of the engine. The tapering rear

styling is typical of Pininfarina's work at the time. In this car, you see traces of Pininfarina's Alfa Romeo Superflow show car, and of the more commonplace Giulia Duetto roadster.

That tendency to reuse and adapt the same styling ideas on multiple cars was quite usual for the great Turin design house. Almost identical sedan shapes were applied to creations for long-term clients such as Peugeot and the British Motor Corporation, whose various makes included Austin, Morris, Riley, and Wolseley. The spectacular Corvette C2-based Rondine was later recapitulated in many of the lines of the modest Fiat 124 Spider, and the Lancia Gamma coupe was transmuted into the Cadillac Allanté. But no variant with the basic early 1960s flowing, unbroken lines of Pininfarina's styling concept is as majestic, impressive, and magnificent as the Superamerica Aerodinamica.

Very few of these big engine cars were produced, and they cost far more than even a coachbuilt Rolls-Royce when new. Potential owners needed the approval of *Il Commendatore*—Enzo Ferrari himself—to even be allowed to proffer funds toward a purchase. Each and every one of these cars was made by the supreme design houses, and they were intimately related to Ferrari's legendary racing cars. All these factors mean that every one of these cars still in existence is now valued at a hundred (or even multiples of a hundred) times above its initial cost, and the examples with special provenance carry yet more value. The first owner of the car on display at the Frist was Felice Riva, whose family produced luxurious motorboats and yachts. The vehicle remained in the possession of the Riva clan until 1977. **RC**

Chrysler Turbine Car

COLLECTION OF FCA, AUBURN HILLS, MICHIGAN

In a bold venture, Carrozzeria Ghia built the bodies for fifty-five experimental Chryslers fitted with gas turbine engines during the early 1960s. Designed internally by Chrysler Corporation in the late 1950s, the multifuel turbine engine was the focus of a long-range development program that ran for decades and cost millions of dollars at a time when a million meant something to major manufacturers. The program was quite serious, with the goal of Chrysler eventually producing the engines, although there was never really much hope of reducing their cost to that of brutal and relatively simple cast-iron piston engines, given the exotic materials required.

Styling of the Turbine bodies was an amalgam of American and Italian ideas—mostly the former. Ghia's technical director, Giovanni Savonuzzi, the brilliant engineer who had almost single-handedly created the postwar design idiom known as the "Italian line" with his Cisitalia racing coupes, might have contributed a bit of input to the cars, but the overall effect was clearly contemporary American. In fact, this project marked the end of Savonuzzi's career as a leading body designer. He was enlisted to head the turbine engine program in Detroit and later became Chrysler's chief research engineer, holding that post until 1968, when he returned to Turin.

Truth be told, Chrysler's Turbine Cars looked like Fords, totally divorced from the dramatic, tall tail fin shape characteristic of late 1950s Ghia-inspired Chryslers. Elwood Engel was hired from Ford to become Chrysler's design chief, and he insisted on exploiting ideas he had espoused in Dearborn. The squared-up Thunderbird-like upper structure of the experimental cars was a strong sign that Ghia's long-term interest in aerodynamics had no place in the Turbine program. The full-width grille was similar to that of the 1961 Lincoln, but neither as elegant nor as well integrated. The high, straight fender line, extending from oversized headlamp bezels (used on Dodge vans later in the 1960s), tapered downward a bit to the taillight surround chrome trim. Numerous internal design cues reflect the turbine theme. Where there *might* be a bit of Ghia influence is in the profile of the curved sill, which barely rises to the rear. The Turbine was an Italian-bodied American car.

There were five Ghia-built prototypes, followed by fifty cars that were identical in color, trim, and mechanical specification and tested for extended periods by a few hundred ordinary American families whose drivers gathered a wealth of useful data. After this unusual program, which was never repeated, six cars were given to museums, with engines rendered inoperative. Chrysler kept three, and the rest were destroyed. It was bandied about that the company had imported the cars without paying customs duties, which reportedly would have been prohibitive. Knowing what it cost to build cars in Italy in the 1960s, and to ship them—I produced and delivered a running one-off in 1966 for about $10,000, a total that covered not only the complete chassis but also the duties—I can tell you that the tariff for the Turbines would have been negligible. The real reason Chrysler destroyed them was to avoid eventual liability and the burden of providing maintenance support. This is not an unusual practice. GM took back all the EV-1 electric prototypes it had leased, and in 2003 crushed them. When the 1973 fuel crisis occurred, Citroën bought back and destroyed all the GS Birotor Wankel–engine sedans it had sold to retail customers.

In 2008 comedian Jay Leno purchased a Turbine Car from the Walter P. Chrysler Museum.[1] I enjoyed a revelatory run in it a couple of years ago: it pretty much felt like riding in any 1960s American car, except for the absence of vibration and the presence of the exotic sound track. The ride was smooth. The noise was at a low level but very definitely different, featuring the high whine of a jet plane taxiing. There was a slight whiff of fuel, again rather like what one might sense in an older airliner. Acceleration was not impressive in any sense—neither noticeably quick nor slow; it was just in line with a typical family car of that era, but throttle response was slower.

Turbines do not make nitrous oxide pollutants, and one day may become the ideal auxiliary power source for electric cars, but we are unlikely to ever again see a car with turbines driving the wheels directly. That's too bad. It was a tantalizing possibility.

Ironically, the company started in the Roaring Twenties by Walter P. Chrysler is now Italian owned: Fiat Chrysler Automobiles. **RC**

1.   Jay Leno, "Jay Leno Drives One of the Last Chrysler Turbines," *Popular Mechanics*, April 11, 2011, www.popularmechanics.com/cars/a11786/jay-leno-drives-one-of-the-last-chrysler-turbines/

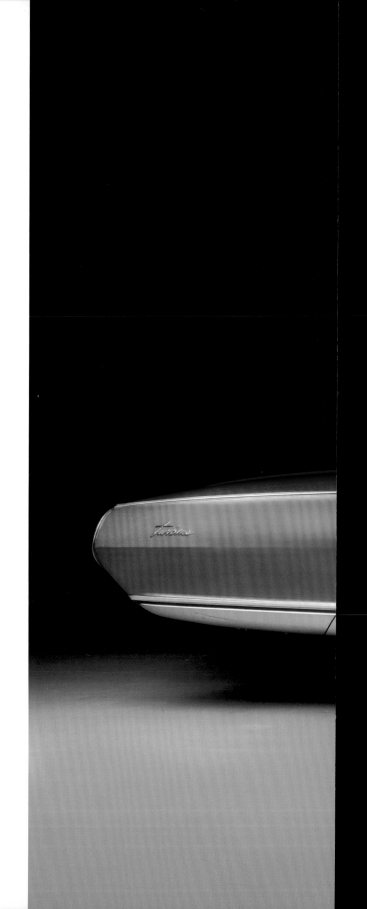

ONE
OF A KIND

Alfa Romeo 6C 2500 S

COLLECTION OF CHRISTOPHER OHRSTROM, THE PLAINS, VIRGINIA

Some of the greatest Alfa Romeo racing and road-going models were built before World War II. The 1930s witnessed the success of Scuderia Ferrari, the company's powerful racing team, managed by Enzo Ferrari and starring drivers such as Giuseppe Campari, Luigi Chinetti Sr., Giuseppe "Nino" Farina, Tazio Nuvolari, and Achille Varzi. Production cars included the sublimely sexy and supercharged 8C 2300 and 8C 2900 classics.

In 1939 Alfa Romeo introduced its 6C 2500, which was built in cabriolet, coupe, *berlina* (five-passenger coupe), and sedan formats. Despite the outbreak of hostilities, a few examples were built as late as 1943 from leftover prewar components, but only for high-ranking military and civilian clients.

This bespoke 6C 2500 S was commissioned in 1946 by a wealthy Milanese woman, Giuliana Tortoli di Cuccioli. Gian Battista "Pinin" Farina had twenty-eight 6C 2500 chassis delivered from Alfa during World War II as part of his wartime contracts. Fourteen were delivered in 1942 and only six of those have survived to the present day. Pinin Farina used one of these chassis to craft this one-off car. The design has been attributed to both Pietro Frua and Giovanni Michelotti.

When completed, the cabriolet was taken on a tour. With the car on loan from Tortoli, Pinin Farina started at the Geneva Motor Show in September 1946. The Alfa was then displayed at the Esplanade de Montbenon in Lausanne, Switzerland, in early October. It then unexpectedly appeared at the Paris Salon.[1] For political reasons, Italian carrozzerie had been barred from exhibiting at the Paris Salon, but Pinin Farina himself piloted the Alfa and his son Sergio drove a custom Lancia Aprilia on a fifteen-hour run from Turin to Paris. On arrival, they washed both cars and parked them in front of the Salon for all to see. The French press raved, "Ce diable de Farina a ouvert son anti-salon personnel!" (This devil Farina has opened his own personal anti-Salon!). But the directors of the Salon responded favorably to the stunt and allowed Pinin Farina to participate in the next Salon.[2]

The Alfa was next exhibited at the 11th Turin Concours d'Elegance. It won the Automobile Club of Italy cup for "Best Open Car." The next year, at the 29th Concours d'Elegance de Monte Carlo, the Alfa received the Grand Prix d'Honneur. It was the subject of numerous magazine and newspaper articles through 1947. That year, Pinin Farina purchased it from Tortoli and used it as his personal car for six months. In 1948 he sold the car to Leonard Lord, CEO of the Austin Motor Company, where it was used as the basis of the design for the Austin A90 Atlantic.[3]

Holden "Bob" Koto, a protégé of Raymond Loewy and a designer on Loewy's staff, originated the design for the famous Studebaker "spinner" nose and helped with the design of the 1949 Ford. He bought the Alfa and in 1950 imported it to the United States. He gave *Hemmings Motor News* these recollections:

> Loewy was always a great person to work for—very considerate and polite. He had offices in Paris, Sao Paolo, London plus a large office in New York and our branch in South Bend. In the early Fifties, he landed a contract with what's now British Leyland to design a new Austin 7. So I went to England for a four-month assignment to Austin—the managing director was Mr. Harriman. . . . I first did a quarter size model, then went full scale on the new Austin. . . . One day Harriman called me into his office and said, "I hear you've been admiring our Alfa." He had used it as his personal car for a few years, and it had been shown in the Geneva auto show. The Austin people had bought it to help develop their Atlantic model.
>
> I saw the Alfa there and expressed a desire to buy it. Harriman told me, "Well, we've decided to give this car to you for a bonus." They didn't exactly give it to me, though— they sold it to me for $2,800 or $1000. It was a bargain even at that, because Harriman said it was actually worth about $9,000. I drove it for a year and eventually sold it over here for $5,000. I won first prize at the Indiana Sports Car Show with it one year and got $400 plus a big trophy.[4]

During the car's trip to America, stevedores fastened hooks and chains to the bumpers to unload the vehicle, subsequently damaging the bodywork. Loewy repaired the car, changing its metallic champagne color to a bright metallic green. James Kent of St. Louis purchased it in 1954 from Koto. After three American owners, the Alfa ended up in the Hill and Vaughn restoration shop in California, where it was disassembled and subsequently purchased as a project by a Japanese businessman, who later sold it to Christopher Ohrstrom. Completely restored by the Guild of Automotive Restorers over a six-year period, it appeared at the 2014 Pebble Beach Concours d'Elegance, as well as at Villa d'Este in 2015, where it was awarded the Trofeo Foglizzo for "Most Beautiful Interior." **KG**

1. David Grainger and Christopher Ohrstrom, *1942/1946 Alfa Romeo 6C-2500 Cabriolet Speciale Coachwork* [restoration book] (Bradford, Ontario: privately printed, 2014), 1–10.

2. Ibid., 2.

3. Ibid., 3.

4. Quoted in ibid., 3–4.

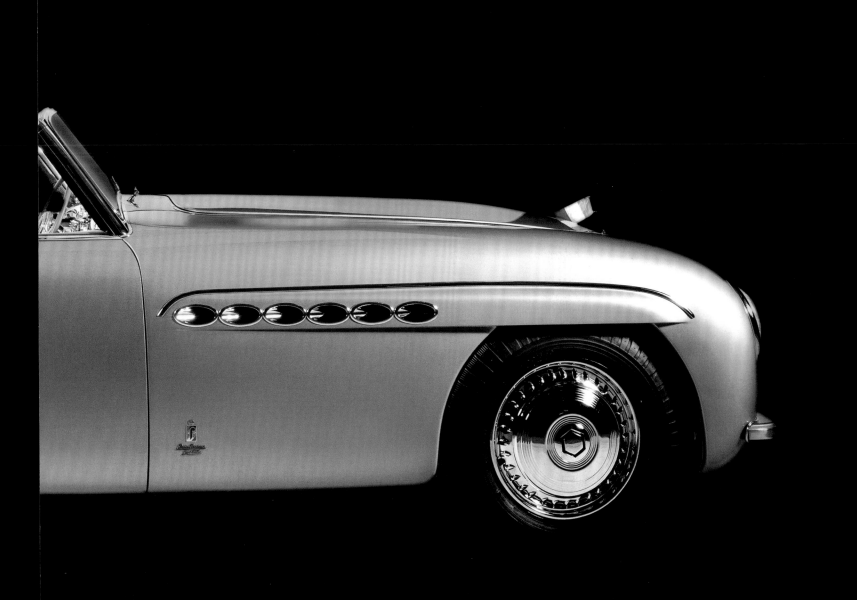

Maserati A6G 2000 Zagato

COLLECTION OF DAVID SYDORICK, BEVERLY HILLS, CALIFORNIA

In 1914 five of the six surviving Maserati brothers started their eponymous automobile company. Race-minded from the outset, Alfieri II, Bindo, Carlo, Ernesto, and Ettore Maserati confidently competed against Alfa Romeo, Lancia, and a host of others, often with an inferior budget but never with lesser machinery. Maserati's bold badge bore a likeness of Neptune's trident, influenced by a towering statue of the Roman sea god in the Piazza Maggiore, a square in the company's home city of Bologna. Alfieri Maserati won the grueling 1926 Targa Florio in Sicily in one of the firm's Tipo 26 race cars.

In 1939 and again in 1940, a Maserati 8CTF driven by Wilbur Shaw convincingly won the Indianapolis 500. The Adolfo Orsi family purchased Maserati in 1940 and moved its operations to Modena.

After World War II ended, Maserati offered a stunning Pinin Farina–designed A6G berlinetta, with newly fashionable slab sides on its alloy body, a flat hood, a close-coupled cabin with a low roofline, a 1,500 cc SOHC six-cylinder engine, and enough power to make driving it entertaining. In 1951 the A6 was upgraded to two liters, with three Weber carburetors. Its additional thirty-five bhp yielded a one hundred mph top speed, depending on the choice of rear axle ratio and lightweight coachwork. Only sixteen examples were sold, each with individual custom coachwork by Frua, Pinin Farina, and Vignale.

For 1954 Maserati based the new A6G 2000 on its A6GCS sports-racing model. The first series cars featured a slightly detuned DOHC two-liter six-cylinder racing engine, developing 150 bhp. Later cars had larger Webers and dual ignition for 160 bhp. Maserati did not build its own bodies. Carrozzeria Pinin Farina was occupied with Ferrari's expanding needs, so Allemano, Frua, and Zagato were tapped to provide custom coachwork. Zagato built one spider for the 1955 Geneva Motor Show and twenty examples with coupe bodies. Frua built seventeen spiders and coupes. Allemano's output was twenty-one units, all of them coupes in various styles. Some fifty-nine A6Gs were made in total, making this a rare car today.[1]

Carrozzeria Zagato, in Milan, specialized in low, lightweight, race-inspired, and curvaceous coachwork.

Zagato-bodied A6G models competed in Gran Turismo (GT) racing in Italy from 1955 to 1957, winning the class championship in 1956 over the previously dominant Fiat Otto Vus. Authors Richard Crump and Rob de La Rive Box noted, "This was a classic example of Maserati's ability to transfer the best qualities of its competition car into a production model; certainly a case of 'racing improves the breed.'"[2]

Anticipating more success, Maserati wanted to build series production cars in much larger numbers. In 1957 the 3500 GT was initiated, with a 230-bhp, 3.5-liter DOHC I-6. Carrozzeria Touring in Milan built nearly two thousand of these as coupes, and they were sold worldwide. About 350 Touring 3500 GT spiders were built as well. Later models had front disc brakes, five-speed gearboxes, and Lucas fuel injection. Besides Touring, Allemano built four 3500 GT coupes; Bertone crafted a one-off coupe, as did Moretti and Boneschi, and Frua presented a one-off spider. Maserati would continue to offer chassis to custom coachbuilders with its limited-production 5000 GT. But for collectors the A6G remains highly desirable, and this Zagato "double bubble" is the rarest of the rare.[3]

David Sydorick is a California car collector specializing in Zagato-bodied cars, especially those with so-called double-bubble rooflines. He learned that a restorer named Sal DiNatale had purchased a double-bubble A6G, S/N 2121, in 1959 and used it as a daily driver when he lived in California. When DiNatale, a native Sicilian, decided to move back to Sicily, he placed the 1955 Maserati, along with some spare parts

and tools, into a cargo container and shipped it to Italy, where it was stored in a small garage. But DiNatale then decided not to move to Italy. After he and Sydorick became friends, Sydorick was eventually able to negotiate for the sale of the car.[4]

Sydorick went to Italy to retrieve the long-lost Maserati. It had been stored in the village of Sabico, near Catana, in an old barn that was used in the filming of *The Godfather*. The car was complete, but it was in rough condition. Its paint had been stripped, the aluminum body had corroded in some places, and the tires were flat. Making matters even more complicated, there was a steel roll-up door, and a three-foot-high brick wall had been erected between the door and the car as a Sicilian security precaution to prevent theft. Sydorick recalls that the entire village turned out to see the car being unearthed. The brick wall was torn down and the coupe was shipped to the United States. After a thorough three-year restoration, the lovely A6G won its class at the Pebble Beach Concours d'Elegance, and ten years later it again took home first-place honors.[5] **KG**

1. Richard Crump and Rob de la Rive Box, *The Illustrated Maserati Buyer's Guide* (Osceola, WI: Motorbooks, 1984), 28.

2. Ibid., 28–29.

3. Ibid., 34–36.

4. Tom Cotter, *The Cobra in the Barn* (St. Paul, MN: MBI, 2005), 187–89.

5. Ibid., 190–91.

Lancia Stratos HF Zero

THE XJ WANG COLLECTION, NEW YORK, NEW YORK

Pininfarina and Bertone were two of Italy's best recognized and most successful postwar coachbuilders. In the intense competition to win Enzo Ferrari's business, Pininfarina triumphed, becoming the Maranello firm's principal supplier, after Bertone's angular design for the Ferrari 308 GT4 in 1973 was not updated for its 1975 successor, the 308 GTB. The 308 Pininfarina commission was a breakthrough. It heralded a long line of curvaceous Pininfarina-styled Ferrari coupes and spiders.

Both Milanese carrozzerie competed for commissions. At the Salon international de l'automobile de Genève, the Salone dell'automobile di Torino, and other major expositions, they debuted outrageous concept cars to impress the public and to entice automakers into choosing one of them over the other.

In the late 1960s and early 1970s, Pininfarina's spectacular show car efforts for Ferrari—the P5, the 512S Berlinetta, and the ultralow Modulo—received considerable international acclaim. Bertone had countered with the Lamborghini Marzal, the first wedge-shaped concept supercar; the Alfa Romeo Carabo; the Bizzarrini Manta; and the Alfa Romeo Iguana. Carrozzeria Bertone went a step further at Turin in 1970 with the Lancia Stratos HF. Nuccio Bertone reportedly intended to call this impossibly low car "Stratolimite," referring to the limit of the stratosphere, but it soon became popularly known by its internal nickname: Zero.[1]

To challenge Pininfarina, whose designs (excepting the Modulo) tended to be alluringly curvaceous, Bertone produced a very low, sharply chiseled coupe that appeared to have been carved out of a solid block of bronze. Design experts have commented that the Stratos HF Zero was a significant step between the 1968 Alfa Romeo Carabo and the production Lamborghini Countach. Even after more than thirty years, the Stratos remains extremely futuristic looking. Nothing about it was conventional, save for the wheels in all four corners. From the thin strip headlights to the backlit (with eighty-four tiny bulbs) taillights, the Zero presaged many modern dream cars. Marcello Gandini was the Zero's designer. Eugenio Pagliano, responsible for interior design at Bertone, said the Carrozzeria Bertone concept was to see how low a car the firm could successfully build.[2]

Pininfarina's Ferrari Modulo was 93.5 centimeters (36 7/8 inches) high; the Zero was 84 centimeters (33 inches) high. Marcello Gandini told Italian journalist Giancarlo Perini that "the very first Stratos was designed as freely as the Autobianchi Runabout, and it reached

the aim for which it was intended—to establish a bridge between Lancia and Bertone. Having seen the Zero, Lancia asked us to come up with an idea for a new sports car that would go rallying in the world championships."[3]

When the design was completed, Carrozzeria Bertone assembled the Stratos HF Zero from existing Lancia components. Once the height target was established and construction began, a 1.6-liter Lancia Fulvia V-4 engine, along with its front suspension, was obtained, without Lancia's knowledge, from a wrecked Fulvia. The front suspension consisted of a pair of short MacPherson struts; the rear suspension, a double-wishbone/coil-spring setup, was formerly the Fulvia's front suspension. A forty-five-liter fuel tank was positioned alongside the engine, and twin electric fans facilitated cooling. Winston Goodfellow wrote that Bertone "made the car without Lancia's knowledge for fear they would negatively react to its audacious design."[4]

Complementing its dramatically low stance, and aiding this car's unconventional nature, the cockpit was positioned as far forward as possible, with the twin seats positioned between the front wheels. The Zero's steering column could be articulated forward to provide room to access the cabin. Simultaneously, a hydraulic mechanism opened the wide Perspex windscreen, which served as the car's single door. A rubber mat at the bottom of the windshield was the step. A pop-up wiper was hidden beneath the windshield. Occupants could see directly ahead and above—and little else. The instrument panel was offset on the left of the wheel arch. Italian manufacturer Gallino-Hellebore was responsible for the unusual and acrobatic steering wheel. There was even room for a spare tire and a small suitcase.

The Stratos HF Zero received a great deal of positive critical acclaim, particularly from other designers. In 1987 Renault Design executive Serge Van Hove, who worked with Marcello Gandini, wrote in the Italian magazine *Auto & Design* that "what Gandini cares about more than anything else, what makes him unique, is the dreaming." Designer Michael Robinson added, "Match

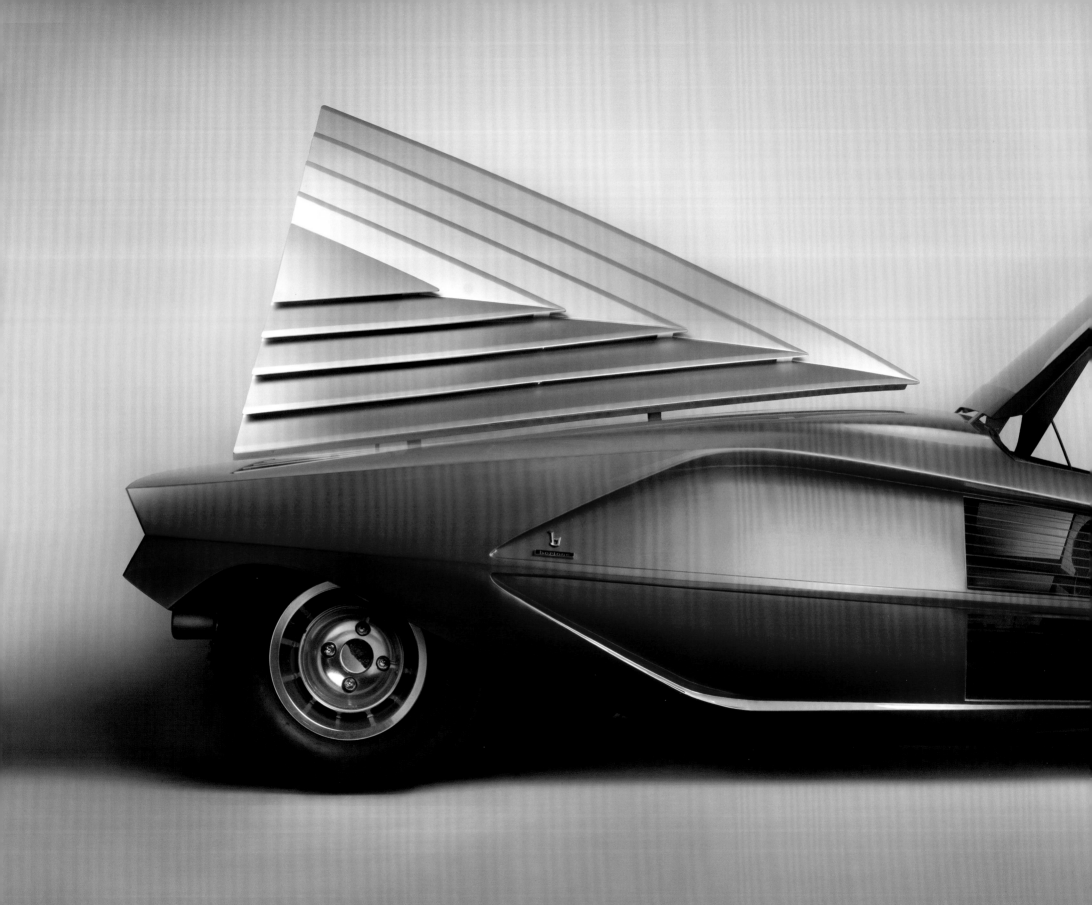

that to Nuccio Bertone's ability to transform dreams into reality, and you have the unrepeatable Stratos Zero."[5]

The cost of building the Zero was reportedly forty million lire (about $450,000 in 1970); a new Lancia Fulvia 1.6 rally coupe was then 2.25 million lire. Some of the Zero's design elements would eventually reach production cars. The squared "chocolate bar" pattern of the seats would appear on the later Lamborghini Countach. In 1971 *Quattroruote*'s editor drove the show car from Milan's beltway into the center of the city to the world-famous Duomo, a feat that took a brave driver, as the Stratos was arguably low enough to be driven right under a semitrailer.

Nuccio Bertone drove the Stratos on public roads to Lancia's offices, dazzling all who saw the impossibly low coupe, and marveling at it himself when he drove it *under* the closed entrance barriers at Lancia's racing department. The result of that meeting was the radical Lancia Stratos rally car. Although the production Lancia Stratos, with its midmounted Fiat/Ferrari V-6 engine, did not closely resemble the Zero, the edgy, all-wheel-drive race car would probably not have been built had it not been for the influence of the inimitable Zero. **KG**

1. Larry Edsall, *Concept Cars: From the 1930s to the Present* (New York: Fall River Press, 2009), 62–64.

2. *Villa d'Este Auction* catalogue (Italy: RM Auctions, 2011).

3. Ibid.

4. Winston Goodfellow, *Italian Sports Cars* (Osceola, WI: MBI, 2000), 106–8.

5. Quoted by Michael Robinson in *Villa d'Este Auction*.

MID-ENGINE

ATS 2500 GT

Imagine the shock waves that would have gone through the business world if, during Steve Jobs's last tenure at Apple, a number of his highest-placed personnel had left en masse. Whatever that reaction might have been, it would have paled compared to the one that hit Italy in November 1961. That's when eight of Enzo Ferrari's top lieutenants left in an episode known as "The Purge" or "The Walkout," depending on who is telling the story.

That mass exodus is worthy of a lengthy discourse unto itself, but the punch line is that the booming Gran Turismo industry quickly became much more exciting when those ex-employees' considerable engineering and management talent suddenly hit the marketplace. Within two years, their fingerprints were all over new sports and GT cars.

ATS was the most ambitious of the new startups and the first beneficiary of all that talent. The name stood for Automobili Turismo e Sport, and its objective was simple: to beat Ferrari on the racetrack and the streets. Three extremely wealthy Ferrari clients backed the effort, and within a matter of weeks of ATS's formation, former Ferrari chief engineer Carlo Chiti was hard at work, creating a proper dual-purpose (road/racing) car.

While at Ferrari, Chiti had been a huge proponent of the mid-engine configuration, where the engine is placed behind the driver and situated around the rear axle. Not only does a central engine offer optimal weight distribution for superior cornering, it also allows for a more aerodynamic shape, as the designer no longer has to battle the height and mass of an engine up front.

Despite those obvious advantages, Enzo Ferrari himself remained unconvinced, saying that the ox should be in front of the cart, not behind it. At ATS, that problematic ox didn't exist, so Chiti designed an all-new, centrally mounted 2.5-liter V-8. The compact power plant was mated to a five-speed transmission, and a fresh new tubular chassis benefited from an all-new suspension system that was independent front and rear.

In one fell swoop, that modern technology allowed ATS to leapfrog over Ferrari and everyone else with a 150-mph machine that would briefly be the world's most sophisticated road car. With minor modifications, it would be competitive on the track—at least, that was the plan.

With the mechanics determined, the coachwork became paramount. From battles inside Ferrari he had witnessed, Chiti knew that Pininfarina had long wanted to do a mid-engine Ferrari, but the famed design house was off limits to ATS because the relationship between Enzo and the father-son duo of Battista and Sergio Pininfarina was too strong.

So ATS settled on what appeared to be the next best thing, the flamboyant Franco Scaglione. Then in his mid-forties, Scaglione had been the chief stylist (as designers were known back then) at Pininfarina's crosstown rival Carrozzeria Bertone. Scaglione's career at Bertone had begun in 1952, and over the next seven years he and company president Nuccio Bertone had created the spectacular Alfa Romeo BAT 5, 7, and 9 design studies, the influential Alfa Giulietta Sprint, and the sensational Sportiva.

After Scaglione left Bertone in 1959, he set up his own design studio. When ATS came calling, his organization was not yet capable of making car bodies, so Carrozzeria Allemano created the coachwork. Largely overlooked today, Serafino Allemano's firm was one of Italy's established coachbuilders during the early 1960s, having opened its doors in 1927. The company had flourished

after World War II, providing coachwork for Ferrari's first-ever Mille Miglia winner, among other projects.

The ATS 2500 GT broke cover to great fanfare at 1963's Geneva Motor Show; in fact, the ATS in the Frist Center exhibition is that exact car. At that world debut, chassis 1001 had two ridges running down the front decklid. The ridges reflected Scaglione's artistic side, for they served no purpose other than ornamentation for additional eye appeal.

Some time after the show, chassis 1001 was repainted a different color, and those ridges were removed for subsequent motor shows. This way, ATS appeared to be producing additional cars, when in fact it was not. Within weeks of the company's formation, friction between the three shareholders (Count Giovanni Volpi, tin magnate Jaime Ortiz Patino, and industrialist Giorgio Billi) had surfaced and quickly worsened. Billi eventually bought out Volpi and Patino but lacked the financial resources to tackle Formula 1, endurance racing, and road car production, and ATS ceased operations in late 1964.

Despite being the first Italian company and GT constructor in general to produce a mid-engine road car, the ATS firm and its impressive 2500 GT are simply footnotes in automotive history. Though ATS had been at the vanguard, the mid-engine road car was truly "born" at 1966's Geneva Motor Show with the unveiling of Lamborghini's astounding Miura. **WG**

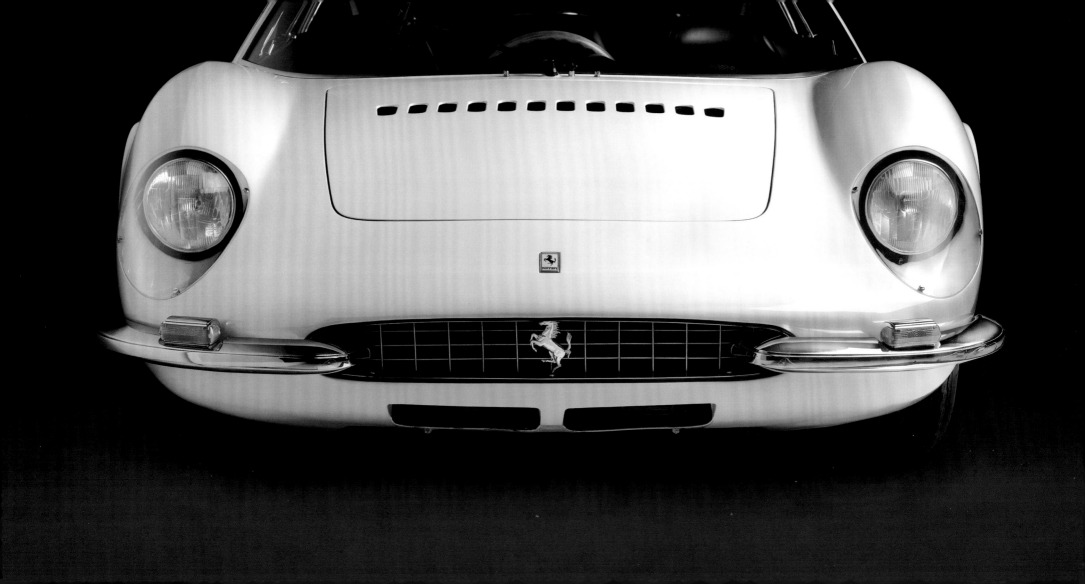

Ferrari 365 P Tre Posti

COLLECTION OF THE LUIGI CHINETTI TRUST, STUART, FLORIDA

Legendary automaker Enzo Ferrari had firm ideas. Although his company successfully raced rear-engine Grand Prix and sports prototype cars, he was convinced that powerful mid-engine cars for the road were simply "too dangerous" for private customers. But coachbuilder Sergio Pininfarina strongly believed that mid-engine production models would be the next important GT car trend, so when he succeeded his father as Ferrari's chief builder of road-going models, he initiated a bold design study to convince the company of their merits.

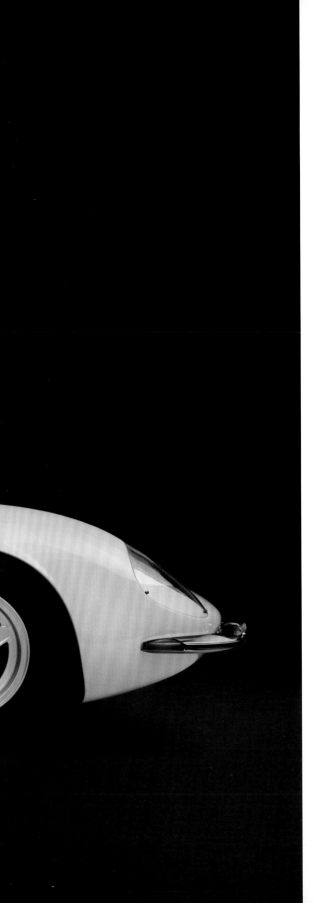

The stunning result was the Ferrari 365 P Tre Posti, Ferrari's first full-sized twelve-cylinder road car, with seats for two passengers located alongside and slightly behind the center driver's seat. A centralized steering wheel and similarly located instruments and controls provided a high level of driver visibility and anticipated the modern McLaren F1.

Aldo Brovarone told author Winston Goodfellow, "I had a completely free hand in designing the car, and the inspiration came from the Berlinetta Dino," a smaller 1965 *speciale*. "I made the shape larger and used the front of the 500 Superfast."[1]

The Tre Posti is replete with iconic Ferrari styling cues, such as an oval-shaped egg-crate grille and Perspex-covered headlamps. Twin flying buttresses evoke the Dino, but as this car is considerably wider, its proportions differ noticeably. Another unusual feature, a large transparent roof section, was formed from athermic, UV-coated, bronze-tinted glass. A subtle reveal connects the two wheel wells and separates the halves of the body. This indentation, which resembles the famed "blood trough" side spear on the Ferrari 365 GTB/4 Daytona, makes this already low-slung car look even lower.

The curved glass window behind the passenger compartment became a feature on Ferrari production cars, as did the taillight assemblies with their triple circular lights. The single large windscreen wiper and five-spoke cast alloy wheels originated on Ferrari race cars. From the outset, the Tre Posti was designed to be a functioning, road-going berlinetta. Inside, it was furnished with a three-spoke wood-rimmed steering wheel, electrically operated windows, black long-grain leather upholstery, and bright red carpets.

The engine is a SOHC, twenty-four-valve, 4.4-liter Ferrari V-12, developing 380 bhp, backed by a five-speed manual transaxle. Competition features include an integrated chrome roll bar, an outside fuel filter, five-spoke cast alloy wheels, a competition pedal box, and a gated shifter. The Tre Posti's vented engine cover, hinged at the rear of the roof, behind the passenger headrests, is topped with a sculpted, polished air intake for the three

Weber carburetors. The suspension consists of independent double wishbones at the front and rear, reminiscent of a Ferrari GT racer.

This car, S/N (serial number) 8971, was a hit at the 1966 Paris Auto Salon, and it was subsequently displayed at the Los Angeles Auto Show. It was then purchased by Luigi Chinetti Sr., a three-time winner of the 24 Hours of Le Mans and the founder of Ferrari in North America. Two invoices came with the car, one from Pininfarina, the other from Ferrari S.p.A. They totaled $26,000, a rather large sum for that era. A second example, S/N 8815, was built for Gianni Agnelli, the head of the Fiat automobile empire.

Luigi Chinetti Jr., who owns the Tre Posti, noted that it "was a real statement from Pininfarina. It was a groundbreaking design in its day and it was the show car in 1966 and 1967. The car was a very big deal at the time—it was pictured in all the magazines. Think of what else was on the road in 1966, and here was this ultramodern, 180+ mph, three-seat Ferrari with a V-12 engine in the middle. There was nothing else like it. It was truly a Formula 1 car for the road. Had Ferrari built it, nobody would ever have given a second thought to the Miura."[2]

Lamborghini began production of its mid-engine Miura in 1967, but Ferrari clung to front-engine cars for several more years. The first full-sized mid-engine roadgoing Ferrari—albeit with an all-new horizontally opposed twelve-cylinder "boxer" engine—was shown in Turin in 1971, and the production model, called the 365 GT4/BB, finally appeared in 1974. McLaren's F1 Supercar—a road-going sports coupe with central steering—took its first bow in 1992, more than twenty-five years after Sergio Pininfarina first proved that Ferrari should build powerful cars for public roads with the sensational Tre Posti. **KG**

1. Winston Goodfellow, *Ferrari Hypercars* (Minneapolis: Motorbooks, 2014), 73.

2. Gooding and Company, "1966 Ferrari 365 P Berlinetta Speciale, Tre Posti," Pebble Beach 2014 auction catalogue (Santa Monica, CA: Gooding and Company, 2014), 12–16.

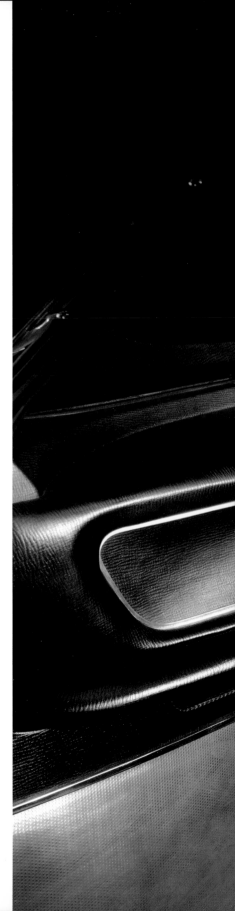

Bizzarrini 5300 Strada

COLLECTION OF DON AND DIANE MELUZIO, YORK, PENNSYLVANIA

A rampant dream in the 1950s and 1960s among many automotive enthusiasts was that of producing one's own car—preferably a high-performance machine with arresting styling. That intense yearning was global, possessing young entrepreneurs such as Californian Milt Brown (engineer of the Apollo adventure) and deep-pocketed Italian industrialists such as Renzo Rivolta and Ferruccio Lamborghini.

Such lofty aspirations likely peaked in the 1960s, when a new GT constructor seemed to appear every month. Of course, new models needed proper engineering and development, and the go-to person many utilized was Giotto Bizzarrini. The talented, fiery engineer was responsible for several of Ferrari's most highly acclaimed models (such as the championship-winning 250 Testa Rossa and 250 GTO, to name just two), and was one of the individuals who left Enzo's company in the infamous row of 1961. He first went to work with ATS and then set up his own consultancy, where his clients included the aforementioned Signori Lamborghini and Rivolta.

With Rivolta, the founder of Iso, Bizzarrini was key to developing the ambitious, Corvette-powered Iso Rivolta GT 2+2 that debuted in 1962. The following year, he put his own stamp on the model that truly brought Iso lasting fame, the legendary two-seat Grifo.

This is where our story gets really intriguing, for Bizzarrini's concept of what the Grifo should look like and ultimately do was vastly different from patriarch Renzo Rivolta's. While Rivolta wanted a comfortable high-performance GT to take on the best from Ferrari, Maserati, and Aston, Bizzarrini envisioned a different future for the vehicle: "From the day I was hired, I pushed him to go racing," the engineer remembered. "I used to say, 'Even though you have a large contract [to purchase Isos] from America, you must be careful. To sell cars with the Iso trademark against Ferrari is impossible,'" Bizzarrini added that, at the end of his consultancy, "Rivolta gave me a chassis and said, 'Here, now you can go make the racing car yourself.'"[1]

That's exactly what Bizzarrini did. That car, along with Iso's own Grifo, debuted at 1963's Turin Auto Show.

Iso's version was known as the Iso Grifo A3/L, and it was sleek, elegant, and luxurious. Its long hood and flowing fastback perfectly characterized what became known as "the Italian look."

Bizzarrini's statement was the Iso Grifo A3/C (the "C" for *Competizione*, "competition"). It had an aggressive shape with a sharp, pointed nose and low roofline so it would cut through the air like an arrow. To make the nose hug the ground, the engineer moved the engine so far behind the front axle that to access the distributor, one had to open a small lid on the top of the dash!

As it had done for Iso's 2+2 GT, Carrozzeria Bertone designed both Grifos. Over the previous decade, the carrozzeria had grown tremendously, thanks to Nuccio Bertone's risk-taking acumen on projects such as Alfa Romeo's seminal Giulietta Sprint. Bertone was also blessed with good taste, a keen eye for design and design talent, and the ability to nurture stylists into industry stars.

Perhaps nothing illustrates these qualities better than the presence of Bertone's young styling chief at the time of the Grifo commission. Giorgetto Giugiaro was just twenty-five, and came from an artistic family of musicians and painters (his grandfather painted frescoes in churches and villas). Amazingly, when Giugiaro began his career at the Fiat styling center in 1956, he didn't know how to drive a car.

"I never felt fulfilled [there]," he recalled years later. "I had to work in silence to learn the trade [and] never knew what happened to my drawings, which was frustrating."[2] Still, Giugiaro's dynamic sketches caught the eye of Bertone, who hired him away from Fiat in 1959.

At that fateful 1963 Turin Show, both Giugiaro-designed Isos were tremendous hits. Bizzarrini sold the first Grifo A3/C on the Iso stand, and immediately started on the second with the proceeds. In total, he would make approximately twenty-five Grifos for Iso in his small workshop in Livorno. After he and Rivolta parted ways in the summer of 1965, he continued producing the cars as the Bizzarrini 5300 Strada. Aside from changing vents and taillight configurations, the Grifo/Strada's radical shape remained basically untouched from 1963 to 1969. Some examples were equipped with a quartet of cross-flow Weber carburetors.

While one might surmise that a form staying the same would make it easy to produce, such was not the case. From the 1947 debut of Pinin Farina's Cisitalia 202 to the early 1960s, the frontline carrozzerias such as Bertone had grown so much that they no longer catered to small clients such as Bizzarrini, who were forced to rely on third-tier coachbuilders that were essentially mom-and-pop operations. According to Bizzarrini, one of the main reasons his company went under was the inability to find a carrozzeria that could regularly and reliably provide the Strada bodies for production.[3]

Despite a few racing successes, the Strada succumbed to manufacturing limitations, only to become an exciting collector car decades later. **WG**

1. Giotto Bizzarrini, interview with the author.

2. Quoted in Winston Goodfellow, *Italian Sports Cars* (Osceola, WI: MBI, 2000), 85.

3. Bizzarrini, interview with the author.

Lamborghini Miura S

COLLECTION OF MORRIE'S CLASSIC CARS, LLC,
LONG LAKE, MINNESOTA

Despite the myths, Ferruccio Lamborghini did *not* start a car company because his Ferrari didn't run well and Enzo Ferrari wouldn't grant him an audience. The wealthy Italian air-conditioner and tractor magnate was convinced that his team could build a better sports car than its rivals. Lamborghini shocked Ferrari and the GT world at the Salone di Torino in 1965 when they presented the chassis for the radical P400 Miura.

Ferruccio's intrepid young engineering trio of Gian Paolo Dallara, Paolo Stanzani, and Bob Wallace had positioned a V-12 engine on the factory floor transversely behind a pair of bucket seats, and suggested to *Il Patrone* that they could build a mid-engine sports car around that configuration. They hoped it would be a racing model.[1]

Coachbuilder Nuccio Bertone reportedly saw the Turin show chassis and told Lamborghini, "I am the one who can make the shoe to fit your foot." Marcello Gandini had succeeded Giorgetto Giugiaro as chief of styling at Bertone in 1965. Bertone had hired Gandini from Marazzi, a small Milanese carrozzeria. Gandini's early sketches for the Miura electrified Lamborghini's engineers. Dallara told Winston Goodfellow, "We immediately realized this was extraordinary, something that happens once in a lifetime." Goodfellow noted that the Miura was termed "*the* show sensation by *Automobile Year*." And Sergio Pininfarina commented wistfully, "When I first saw it, I said, 'I wish I could do that myself.'"[2]

Named for the legendary Spanish fighting bulls originally bred by Don Eduardo Miura Fernández, the low-slung Miura berlinetta shocked onlookers in Monaco when it first appeared. Lamborghini audaciously parked a blood-orange prototype in front of the Hotel de Paris, and stood back while compliments flowed. Overnight, the P400 made everything in the Ferrari road-going car lineup obsolete. It would be years before Ferrari built a full-sized mid-engine sports car for the road. Compared to a bulky Ferrari 365 GTB/4 Daytona, the slender Miura resembled a stiletto on cast magnesium wheels.

The four-liter, 350-bhp, six-carburetor V-12 was transversely mounted, directly behind the seats, as the youthful engineering trio had proposed. The engine and transaxle shared the same oil sump, and the independent double-wishbone suspension front and rear was similar to that of a Formula 1 Grand Prix racer. Gandini told Goodfellow, "The Miura wasn't the creation of a new line. Rather, it was the arrival point of all the sports cars of the 1950s and 1960s. The lines were very soft, very animalistic."[3]

A Miura is a very exciting car to drive. You sink deeply into the bucket seats; the steering is firm, and very direct; the disc brakes are quite good for that era; and the engine roaring away behind a thin sheet of glass, just inches from your ears, makes for exciting motoring. The cockpit is somewhat cramped; the gearlever, in its gated web, takes great effort to operate; and the overall impression is more race car than road car.

The Miura's styling still holds up remarkably well. But there were many problems initially: the engine oil in the first Miura was shared with the transaxle; the early cars were hot inside, and noisy and uncomfortable, with high-speed handling issues. Bob Wallace and his road-test crew had corrected nearly all the faults when the Miura S bowed in 1969, with hotter camshafts, twenty more units of brake horsepower (bhp), ventilated disc brakes, and a top speed of 177 mph. "The Miura was a watershed supercar," says Robert Ross, chief automotive editorial consultant for *Robb Report*. "There is perhaps no stronger icon of the 1960s."[4]

The last Miura variant, the SV (for *Spinto Veloce*, "tuned fast"), had wider bodywork, a more rigid chassis, a split oil sump, fatter rear tires, 385 bhp, and a revised suspension. It was capable of 180 mph. Lamborghini built 465 P400s, 238 400Ss, and 148 SVs. (Some sources say the totals were 475, 140, and 150 respectively.) Only one Miura convertible was produced, but there are several clones. Bob Wallace built a hot-rodded race-spec 440-bhp Miura called the Jota, and the factory subsequently built four replica "Jota" Miuras. The original Wallace Jota was destroyed in a crash.[5]

The Miura changed everything. It put Lamborghini firmly on the map as a serious competitor to hitherto unassailable Ferrari and Maserati. It was a technical tour de force, and its styling still looks contemporary. Lamborghini never planned to race these cars, although a few owners tried.

Years later, Ferruccio Lamborghini himself said, "I still miss the Miura. No one has ever equaled it. When I miss the sound and the fury, I take refuge in my garage and turn the key in the ignition of my Miura. Just long enough to make the needle move."[6]

Successors such as the Countach, Diablo, and Murciélago were even more outrageous, but the Miura represents Lamborghini in its purest iteration. Today, commanding seven-figure prices, the Miura remains the definitive Lamborghini and the premier sports car of its era. **KG**

1. Peter Coltrin and Jean-Francois Marchet, *Lamborghini Miura* (London: Osprey, 1982), 31.

2. Winston Goodfellow, *Italian Sports Cars* (Osceola, WI: Motorbooks, 2000), 95.

3. Ibid., 96.

4. Robert Ross, e-mail to Ken Gross, September 18, 2015.

5. Rob de la Rive Box, *Illustrated Lamborghini Buyer's Guide* (Osceola, WI: Motorbooks, 1983), 42, 48, and 53.

6. Jared Zaugg, *Gentlemen, Start Your Engines!* (Berlin: Gestalten, 2015), 272.

ON TWO WHEELS

Moto Guzzi V-8

COLLECTION OF THE GILBERT FAMILY, LOS ANGELES, CALIFORNIA

From the outset, Moto Guzzi was a force to be reckoned with in the panoply of Italian road-going and racing motorcycles. The company was conceived by two Italian air force pilots and their mechanic just before the end of World War I. One of the pilots, Carlo Guzzi, provided the engineering; the other pilot, Giorgio Parodi, came from a family of shipbuilders and financed the venture. Giovanni Ravelli, the mechanic, would have been the racer.

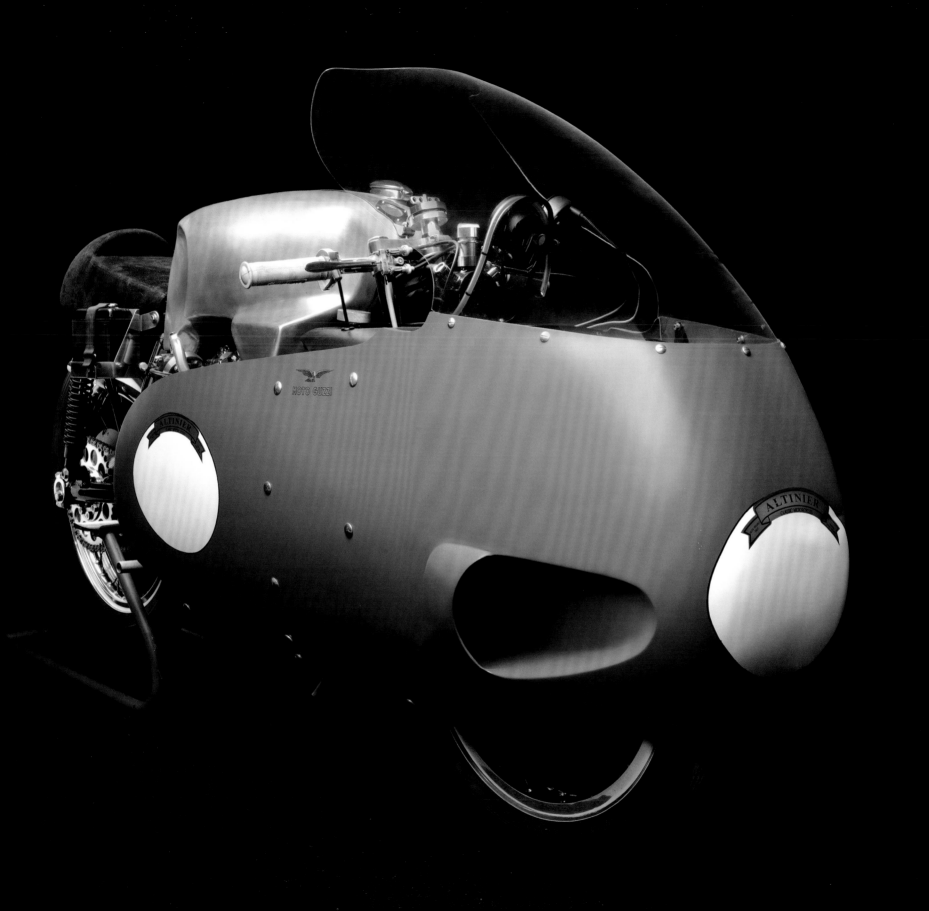

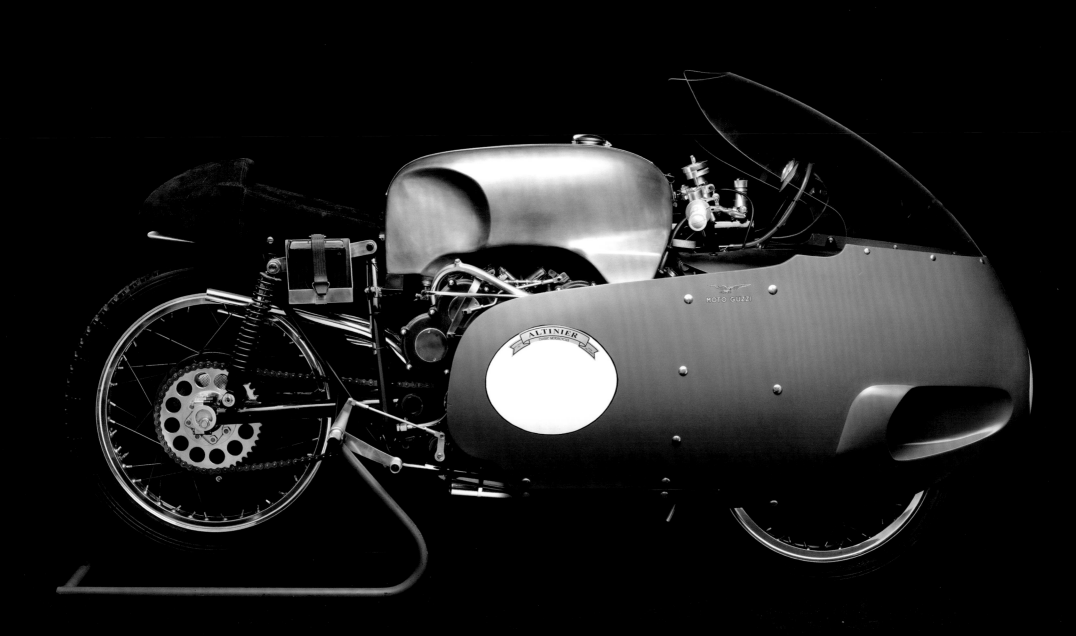

Unfortunately, Ravelli died in a crash just after the war ended, and the wings that have always appeared on the Guzzi badge are in his memory. The company was established in 1921.

Unlike their counterparts who settled on one engine configuration and repeated the practice, Guzzi's bold engineers knew no boundaries. Their projects ranged from a horizontal single-cylinder setup featuring an exposed flywheel (popularly known as the "baloney slicer") to both in-line and transverse V-twins, as well as horizontal and in-line triples and fours. Guzzis were known for innovation, power, variety, and reliability. Complexity never daunted Guzzi engineers. That fact was hardly in doubt with the marque's most radical machine, the 1955 V-8, which also became known as the Otto.

As Guzzi's head of engineering, Dr. Giulio Carcano was responsible for the Otto, assisted by Enrico Cantoni, Umberto Todero, and racing team stalwarts Ken Kavanagh and Fergus Anderson. It was Anderson who first released a drawing of the Otto to the world motorcycle press, in an announcement that revealed Moto Guzzi's plans for the 1955 Grand Prix competition season. Anderson challenged recipients to guess the number of cylinders. As the radical engine was largely hidden by a streamlined "dustbin" fairing, this was impossible to determine.

Carcano's brainchild was a miniature, over-square (44 x 41 mm), 500 cc (30.5-cid, or cubic inch displacement) V-8, with dual overhead camshafts and a petite 20 mm Dell'Orto single-barrel carburetor for each of its eight tiny cylinders. And, it was water cooled, so a small radiator was an integral part of the package. The complete engine weighed just 45 kilograms (about 99 pounds) and the entire motorcycle weighed only 148 kilograms (326 pounds). Competitive, highly tuned Grand Prix Norton Manx 500 cc bikes from England in the same period had an output of about fifty bhp. The Guzzi V-8 developed a remarkable seventy-eight bhp at twelve thousand rpm (revolutions per minute).

Even more impressive, the Guzzi V-8's top end, with tall gearing, was 172 mph, an unheard-of speed in that era for a racing motorbike, and about as fast as most Grand Prix (GP) cars. Depending on the track requirement, the Otto could be had with four, five, or six forward speeds. Dustbin fairings were controversial. They definitely reduced wind resistance, but machines fitted with them could become unstable at high speeds, leading to violent crashes. Also, racing motorcycles in this era suffered from primitive suspensions and drum brakes that were prone to early fading. Despite the radiator, these engines ran hot and were liable to seize up midrace, magnifying the danger to the riders.

Guzzi V-8s were fast qualifiers and they often led races, but they suffered some truly spectacular crashes before the concept could be fully developed. Fergus Anderson reportedly crashed one during initial testing at Modena. British riding great Bill Lomas tumbled off an Otto and suffered head injuries at the 1956 Senigallia GP, in Ancona, Italy. Ace rider Ken Kavanagh simply refused to ride an Otto again after the 1956 Belgian GP at the ultrahigh-speed Spa-Francorchamps track. Sadly, Guzzi and several other manufacturers withdrew from GP competition in 1957, so development of this high-potential combination came to a halt. Speeds of 170 mph plus were unattainable in motorcycle GP racing until the early 1970s, attesting to how advanced the Otto was for its time.

While a number of manufacturers have tried dustbins, there's arguably never been a better-looking midcentury GP racer. The swoopy, humped fuel tank features large cutaways for the rider's knees, the abbreviated seat tapers into a raised tail section to keep the rider snugly positioned, the raucous V-8 engine is almost completely hidden, and there's an organ cluster of eight small exhaust pipes, producing a cacophony of noise you would never expect to hear on a race bike outside of a Honda six-cylinder. *Road & Track*'s Alex Kierstein wrote, "It sounds like eight tiny dragons screaming and spitting fire from within an alloy prison designed by wizards, while being drenched in gasoline."[1] Over time, the Otto has become the stuff of legends.

The Moto Guzzi factory owns two original examples. The bike in the Frist Center exhibition is an exact replica, built using a spare factory V-8 engine and other original parts. We'll likely never see another racing motorcycle as brilliant, complex, and scary as the Moto Guzzi Otto. **KG**

---

1. Alex Kierstein, "500cc Moto Guzzi V8? That's Better than Coffee," *Road & Track*, April 10, 2013, www.roadandtrack.com/car-culture/videos/a4218/better-than-coffee-moto-guzzi-v8/.

MV Agusta 750 Sport

COLLECTION OF PETER MATTHEW CALLES, BETHESDA, MARYLAND

MV Agusta motorcycles for the road were always exclusive and expensive engineering marvels, closely related to the company's Grand Prix racing machines. The initial four-cylinder engine design stemmed from the Gilera Rondine, designed by engineer Pietro Remor. When Remor left Gilera in 1947, to join MV, he brought along the expertise needed to update the design in 1950. MV stands for Meccanica Verghera; the MV Agusta name came about because the company is located in the village of Verghera, Italy, and is owned by the wealthy Agusta family.

The heart of the MV 750 Sport superbike was an engine that could well have powered a diminutive sports car like a Moretti or a Giaur. Giftwrapped in a race-inspired fairing, MV offered a four-cylinder power plant that was transversely mounted, shaft-driven, and air-cooled, with a gear-driven dual overhead camshaft (DOHC). It had a capacity of 742.9 cc. Fed by a quartet of Dell'Orto carburetors, it was capable of 72 bhp at a then-astonishing 9,200 rpm. (Some sources claimed 75 bhp at 8,500 rpm.)

During the middle of the twentieth century, transverse in-line fours in motorcycles were a rare commodity. With its elegant sand-cast cylinder cases and squared cooling fins, the 750 Sport's stunning I-4 resembled a complex mechanical sculpture. Its slightly inclined mounting, tightly embraced by the machine's gracefully shaped tubular frame, was underscored by a curved duo of chromed exhaust pipes on each side, flowing gracefully into Siamese-twin megaphones.

MVs were widely considered to be "the Ferrari of motorcycles," owing to their powerful and complex engines, race-bred handling, extensive application of Italian racing red componentry, and an exhaust note that sent chills up the spines of those within hearing. The 750 Sport and its slightly more powerful successor, the 750 Super Sport, were capable of 135-mph speeds, and despite being limited to duo-duplex drum brakes at first (the best of that era), an enthusiastically ridden 750 Sport could show its heels to nearly every vehicle, on two or four wheels, that it encountered.

The firm's legendary competition riders—men like Giacomo Agostini, John Hartle, Mike Hailwood, Gary Hocking, and John Surtees—won numerous Isle of Man Tourist Trophies (TTs), often at triple-digit averages, in several displacement classes. The view of sleek, fully faired, red-over-gray MVs heeled over in the island's impossibly tight and terrifyingly dangerous turns became almost commonplace. Skilled and wealthy riders demanded road-going copies—the bikes attracted envious crowds wherever they appeared.

Motorcycle writer Jeff Clew noted, "With an incredible number of World Championships to its credit (37), the MV represented the very epitome of Italian motorcycle engineering. . . . The road-going versions of the Grand Prix racers attracted the more discerning purchaser, to whom price was only a secondary consideration."[1]

MV's designers elected to take the bold red, white, and blue of the US flag and paint it dramatically on the bike's tank, seat, frame, and fairing. The lettering was brash and bold, and the "music" from the quad exhaust was magnificent. It's always been said that Honda's later four-cylinder direction emanated from MV's pioneering efforts.

Britain's *Motorcycle Sport* magazine crowed, "Overworked and somehow inadequate words like Character and Presence and Charisma tend to recur in conversations during chance meetings of enthusiasts on the road when the focus of discussions is an MV Agusta 750 Sport. . . . It gets the adrenalin flowing even when hunched in silent majesty on the stand, and it is interesting to see the effect it has on people who would not normally give a motorcycle a second glance. . . . An MV is difficult to ignore."[2]

Road testers confirmed that the Sport was capable of a heady 57 mph in first gear alone. Fifth gear topped out at over 135 mph and the usable rev range was an astonishing 9,500–11,500 rpm—a previously unheard-of achievement in that era. Superlatives abounded: Vic Willoughby, a noted British motorcycle tester in the late 1970s, enthused, "Viewed head on, the MV resembles a charging bull and bristles with menace. Creating an impression of terrific speed, even at rest, it remains unequalled for sporting good looks."[3]

All 750 Sports were shaft-driven, and the rear hub was an attractively finned casting that matched the engine's gray finish. Drum brakes gave way to virtually fade-proof Brembo discs as production wound down in late 1979. The weak point was said to be the bike's multiplate clutch, and a few testers complained that, while on long sweepers the machine's handling was flawless,

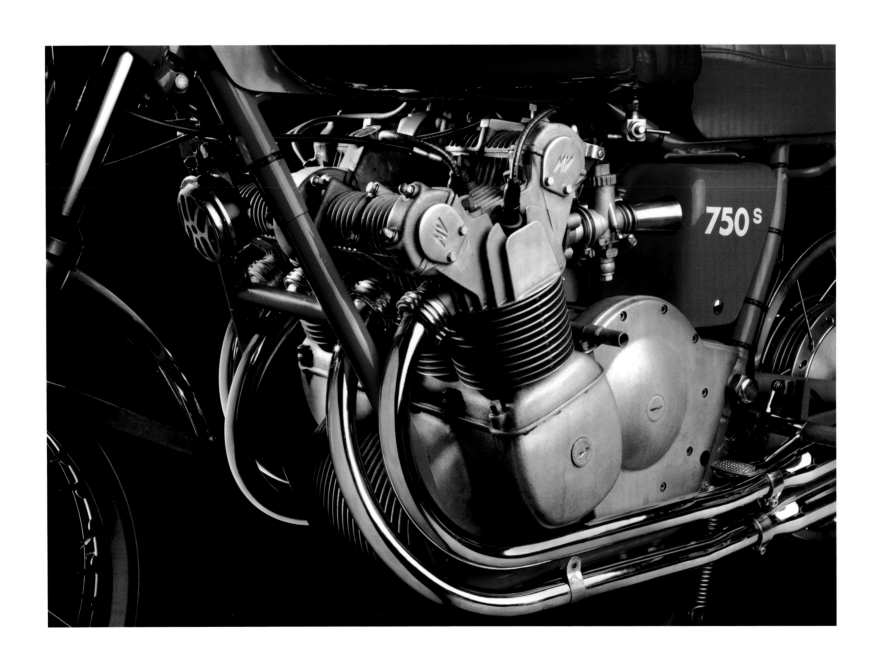

it tended to wobble at lower speeds, possibly because of the weight and balance issues caused by the high-mounted engine.

This was a $6,000 motorcycle in an era when a Ducati 900SS could be had for thousands less. "Nothing about the new MV Agusta 750 S is understated," wrote *Cycle*'s editors. "This red and silver roadster is the center of attention wherever it appears."[4] The same is true today, at any gathering of enthusiasts. Just 150 examples were sold in 1973. When MV ceased building motorcycles in 1979, to concentrate on helicopter production, aficionados—even those who couldn't *begin* to afford one—mourned the passing of an extraordinary machine. **KG**

1. Jeff Clew, *MV Agusta 750S America and Other 750/850 Fours* (Somerset, England: Haynes, 1983), 42.

2. Vic Willoughby, "MV Agusta Sport America: Getting the Adrenalin Flowing," *Motorcycle Sport*, December 1979, 652.

3. Ibid., 654.

4. *Cycle*, May 1975, quoted in Clew, *MV Agusta 750S*, 21.

Ducati 750 Super Sport

COLLECTION OF SOMER AND LOYCE HOOKER, BRENTWOOD, TENNESSEE

In the pantheon of great motorcycle engineers, there's unquestionably a place for the incomparable Fabio Taglioni, chief designer and technical director of Ducati from 1954 to 1989. Taglioni's powerful, lightweight sporting V-twin catapulted the status of the small Bolognese firm from interesting to legendary.

Born in September 1920, Taglioni was nearly fifty years old when his unique designs for desmodromic (mechanically opening and closing) valve gear, perfected on Ducati's small-capacity singles, led to the development of bold, high-revving 750 cc V-twins with competitive capability. Ducati's ascent began with the design of the 750GT, which incorporated the engine as a stressed member. The front cylinder was cleverly positioned between the frame down tubes. The engine's 90-degree L-shaped layout, with both cylinders exposed to the onrushing air, virtually eliminated the common V-twin malady of overheating rear cylinders. From the outset, Marzocchi suspensions, Borrani alloy wheels, and Conti megaphone exhausts made Ducati owners the envy of the café racer set, with Dell'Orto carburetors soon to join the list of top-quality specifications. The even racier, sleekly styled 750 Sport followed, designed by Leopoldo Tartarini of Italjet. The 750 Sport's bright orange finish, optional bikini fairing, clip-on handlebars, Scarab disc brakes, Ceriani forks, and Tomaselli twist grip, along with other constantly improving specifications, encouraged owners to race their machines.

And the best was yet to come. Paul Smart and Bruno Spaggiari won an impressive one-two finish at the first Imola 200 race in April 1972 on factory-special 750s, replete with silver metalflake paint and upswept exhausts. Almost overnight, thanks to their victory at what was called "the Daytona of Europe," Ducati and Taglioni were hailed worldwide, and Ducati galloped to the forefront of performance motorcycle competition. Smart and Spaggiari's machines were equipped with

desmodromic valve gear—the first Ducati twins with that feature, which fed their ability to rev to 8,000 rpm. It was just a matter of time before a production version would appear, such was the clamor for copies.

The new, appropriately named 750 Super Sport weighed just under four hundred pounds. It boasted fully machined billet connecting rods, a bevel-gear camshaft drive, round crankcases, larger valves, triple disc brakes, five-speed gearboxes, and a top speed of nearly 140 mph. Ducati applied to the FIA for homologation and allegedly produced the requisite one hundred examples for certification, but that's not certain. Three of these bikes came to the United States. *Cycle* editor Cook Neilson and his tuner, Phil Schilling, would modify one of these, a "California Hot Rod" 900 cc Imola replica, booting it to a convincing Daytona win in March 1977. Ducati aficionados went wild, and sales in America rose.

Meanwhile, production 750 Super Sports—thinly disguised race-ready machines—became available. They were finished in *azzurro* (a bluish green shade that was also called "duck-egg green") and *alluminio metallizzato*, with sleek, lightweight fiberglass bodywork designed by Tartarini, who was inspired by the Imola racers. The big-humped fuel tank held twenty-four liters, and clear fiberglass strips on the sides allowed riders to check the fuel level. These were quickly nicknamed "green frame" Super Sports.

Some 401 examples were made in total, with Ducati race shop–assembled engines. Later in 1974, the factory offered a racing kit for the 750s with competition camshafts, larger main jets, race fairings, upswept

exhausts, and an oil cooler, as well as the capability to run at 8,800 rpm (with silencers) and even up to 9,200 rpm (with megaphones). Round-case production gave way after 1974 to the later square-case, bevel-drive 750 and 900 Super Sports—nice bikes, to be sure, but not as special as the limited-production, hand-built '74s.

Ducati authority Ian Falloon notes that "for Fabio Taglioni the 750 90-degree L-twin was the perfect engine layout for a motorcycle. Little wider than a single it could be mounted low in the frame for a low centre of gravity, and it provided the best compromise between smoothness, power, and reliability."[1]

Taglioni explained that it was difficult to silence the 750's big cylinders, and said it was hard to build a proper frame: "It is difficult to make it look nice, or as we say, it is not easy to dress. But with regards to looks, it's like women. As we say, you may be seen going about with beautiful women, but in the end you marry your wife!"[2]

The irrepressible Taglioni died in 2001, but not before he'd created some of the greatest motorcycles ever built. Today, the round-case 750 Super Sport is one of the most sought-after Ducati models. Falloon notes that this bike was "the finest motorcycle sporting experience available in 1974."[3] Some forty years later, this fast, beautiful Italian machine can still hold its own. **KG**

1. Ian Falloon, *The Book of the Ducati 750SS* (Dorchester, England: Veloce Publishing, 2010), 45.

2. Ibid.

3. Ibid., 47.

CHECKLIST OF THE EXHIBITION

1946 Alfa Romeo 6C 2500 S

COLLECTION OF CHRISTOPHER
OHRSTROM, THE PLAINS, VIRGINIA

1950 Cisitalia 202 SC

THE REVS INSTITUTE FOR
AUTOMOTIVE RESEARCH, INC.,
NAPLES, FLORIDA

**1952 Cunningham C3
Continental**

THE REVS INSTITUTE FOR
AUTOMOTIVE RESEARCH, INC.,
NAPLES, FLORIDA

**1952 Lancia B52 Aurelia
PF200 Spider**

COLLECTION OF LINDA AND BILL
POPE, PARADISE VALLEY, ARIZONA

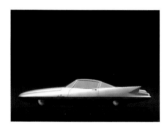

1955 Chrysler Ghia Gilda

COLLECTION OF KATHLEEN
REDMOND AND SCOTT GRUNDFOR,
ARROYO GRANDE, CALIFORNIA

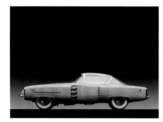

1955 Lincoln Indianapolis

COLLECTION OF JAMES E. PETERSEN
JR., HOUSTON, TEXAS

**1955 Maserati A6G
2000 Zagato**

COLLECTION OF DAVID SYDORICK,
BEVERLY HILLS, CALIFORNIA

1957 Moto Guzzi V-8

COLLECTION OF THE GILBERT
FAMILY, LOS ANGELES, CALIFORNIA

1966 Ferrari 365 P Tre Posti

COLLECTION OF THE LUIGI CHINETTI
TRUST, STUART, FLORIDA

1968 Bizzarrini 5300 Strada

COLLECTION OF DON AND DIANE
MELUZIO, YORK, PENNSYLVANIA

1970 Lamborghini Miura S

COLLECTION OF MORRIE'S CLASSIC
CARS, LLC, LONG LAKE, MINNESOTA

1970 Lancia Stratos HF Zero

THE XJ WANG COLLECTION, NEW
YORK, NEW YORK

1953 Fiat 8V Supersonic

COLLECTION OF PAUL GOULD,
PATTERSON, NEW YORK

1953 Alfa Romeo BAT 5

THE BLACKHAWK COLLECTION,
DANVILLE, CALIFORNIA

1954 Alfa Romeo BAT 7

THE BLACKHAWK COLLECTION,
DANVILLE, CALIFORNIA

1955 Alfa Romeo BAT 9

THE BLACKHAWK COLLECTION,
DANVILLE, CALIFORNIA

**1961 Ferrari 400
Superamerica Pininfarina
Series II Aerodinamico**

COLLECTION OF BERNARD AND
JOAN CARL, WASHINGTON, D.C.

1962 Ferrari 250 GTO

COLLECTION OF BERNARD AND
JOAN CARL, WASHINGTON, D.C.

1963 ATS 2500 GT

COLLECTION OF BERNARD AND
JOAN CARL, WASHINGTON, D.C.

1963 Chrysler Turbine Car

COLLECTION OF FCA, AUBURN
HILLS, MICHIGAN

1973 MV Agusta 750 Sport

COLLECTION OF PETER MATTHEW
CALLES, BETHESDA, MARYLAND

**1974 Ducati 750
Super Sport**

COLLECTION OF SOMER AND LOYCE
HOOKER, BRENTWOOD, TENNESSEE

CONTRIBUTORS

Formerly executive director of the Petersen Automotive Museum in Los Angeles, **KEN GROSS** has curated many exhibitions of extraordinary automobiles for fine art museums, including *The Allure of the Automobile* at Atlanta's High Museum of Art (2010) and the Portland (Oregon) Art Museum (2011); *Speed: The Art of the Performance Automobile* at the Utah Museum of Fine Arts, in Salt Lake City (2012); *Sensuous Steel: Art Deco Automobiles* at Nashville's Frist Center for the Visual Arts (2013); *Porsche by Design: Seducing Speed* at the North Carolina Museum of Art, in Raleigh (2013); and *Dream Cars: Innovative Design, Visionary Ideas* at the High Museum of Art (2014) and the Indianapolis Museum of Art (2015). Forthcoming exhibitions include *Sculpted in Steel: Art Deco Cars and Motorcycles* for the Museum of Fine Arts, Houston.

An award-winning automotive journalist for over forty years, Gross has received the Automotive Hall of Fame's Distinguished Service Citation, the Lorin Tryon Trophy at the Pebble Beach Concours d'Elegance, the Ken Purdy Award from the International Motor Press Association, the Dean Batchelor Lifetime Achievement Award from the Motor Press Guild in Los Angeles, the Lee Iacocca Award, and the International Automotive Media Lifetime Achievement Award from the International Society for Vehicle Preservation.

Along with several exhibition catalogues, Gross's fifteen automotive books include the *Illustrated BMW Buyer's Guide* (1994), *Ferrari 250GT SWB* (1999), *Art of the Hot Rod* (2008), *Hot Rods and Custom Cars: Los Angeles and The Dry Lakes* (2009), *So-Cal Coupe* (2013), *Vintage Cars* (2014), and *Hot Rod Milestones* (2015). Gross cowrote *Rockin' Garages* (2013) with Tom Cotter.

Gross has been a Pebble Beach Concours d'Elegance chief class judge for twenty-six years, and he serves on the selection committee. He has judged at car shows at Amelia Island, St. Michaels, Boca Raton, Radnor Hunt, Keels and Wheels, The Elegance at Hershey, Pinehurst, Forest Grove, the Concours of America at St. Johns, Hilton Head Island, and Rodeo Drive.

An admitted Italophile, he's owned three Ducatis, two Ferraris, and a Lamborghini. Gross lives in Hamilton, Virginia, with his wife, Trish Serratore, president of the National Automotive Technicians Education Foundation (NATEF), and his two children, Jake and Kayla.

ROBERT CUMBERFORD is a design consultant to the automotive and aircraft industries. As a design commentator and critic, he regularly writes for *Automobile* magazine, and since 1987 has been the *opinionista* for *Auto & Design*, a Turin-based journal produced in Italian and English. He has published thousands of articles in half a dozen countries during the past six decades, principally on vehicle design, and has contributed to several books.

Cumberford began his career in 1954 at age nineteen, as a designer for General Motors. He was assigned to the Chevrolet studio before being named the first head of Studio X. In 1957 he began

studying aesthetics at UCLA. He subsequently worked for Albrecht Goertz (New York) and Holman and Moody (Charlotte, North Carolina) before forming Cumberford Design International (CDI) in 1964. With offices in Tuxedo Park, New York; Mexico City; and Northampton, England, CDI served industrial clients and Wall Street investment firms. Its 1972 study of Wankel engine potential remains one of the most accurate assessments of that power plant concept ever produced. Cumberford also worked in Turin from 1965 to 1972 on the construction of several cars built in small shops, and led development of the Martinique luxury sports car as a vice president and design director at Vehicle Development Corporation. He has been an instructor in automobile design at the Art Center College of Design–Europe, in Vevey, Switzerland.

Cumberford moved to France in 1972. Under the auspices of the International Innovations Institute, an offshoot of the Organisation for Economic Co-operation and Development, he was a counselor to the government of the Republic of Madagascar from 1978 to 1979. Internationally respected as an expert and historian, Cumberford has been a judge in the most prestigious automotive Concours d'Elegance in the United States and Europe (including Pebble Beach and Villa d'Este), the Canadian World Automotive Design Competition, and the *Quatro Rodas*/Fiat–sponsored design contest in Brazil.

WINSTON GOODFELLOW is an award-winning automotive writer and photographer who grew up in the San Francisco Bay area. His love affair with the automobile (and particularly Italian cars) was kindled in the mid-1970s when he was in high school. One day after basketball practice, one of his teammates called out, "You have to see this!" Parked next to the gym was a new Ferrari 365 GT4/BB (Berlinetta Boxer) owned by a Saudi prince who attended a nearby college. A few weeks later he saw another prince's Lamborghini Countach LP400, and was forever hooked.

He spent most of the 1980s in the financial services industry, and then changed careers in the early 1990s to become an automotive writer and photographer. When he started on this new path, he thought it best to specialize in what interested him—performance and collector cars, and their history. He soon found himself shooting and driving things that were fast and cool, and spending time with the people who created them. More than once he has commented that it's like being a grown-up kid, with both hands deeply immersed in a very fast cookie jar.

Over the past two-plus decades his words and photos have appeared in more than sixty publications on several continents, and he has authored fourteen books and privately commissioned monographs. His last work, the critically acclaimed *Ferrari Hypercars*, was voted 2014's Book of the Year at the twenty-fourth annual International Automotive Media Competition.

Goodfellow has also been an organizer, chief class judge, and class judge at the world's top concours, including the Pebble Beach Concours d'Elegance, the Concorso d'Eleganza at Villa d'Este in Italy, and The Quail, A Motorsports Gathering. He was on Meguiar's Collector Car Person of the Year selection committee, and served as a seminar leader with the Smithsonian Institution, Washington, D.C. He has also advised numerous collectors on the purchase or sale of their cars, and given them guidance on their collections.

Today, he still feels he's one of the luckiest people in the world, having stumbled onto one of life's great secrets. As he says, "If you love what you do, very rarely is it work!"